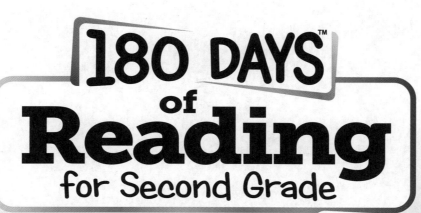

180 DAYS™ of Reading for Second Grade

Name: _____ Date: _____

📖 **As You Read**

Put a heart next to your favorite part(s) of the story.

How Night Came to Be: Part 4

While Bat was gone, Owl and Fox spotted the basket. They wondered what was inside. Fox sniffed it and Owl tried to push it over.

"Should we open it?" Fox asked.

"It is not ours," Owl answered.

But they were so curious, and they could not resist the mystery. They had to open the basket! Together, they lifted the top. Darkness flew out! Owl and Fox watched as it spread all over the sky.

Just then, Bat was on his way back. He gasped upon seeing the open basket.

"What have you done?" he cried, swooping in.

Startled, Owl and Fox ran away. Bat looked around and saw only darkness. He flew and flew trying to gather it up. It will take all night to put it back in the basket! he thought. And there is so much of it! It will never fit back in!

From that time on, Bat had a new job to do. He rested during the [day so] he could work at night. All night, he gathered the darkness and [put it i]n the basket. By morning, it was light again. But the darkness [was] tricky. Each time Bat pushed the last bit into the basket, the other end of the basket cracked open. Darkness slowly escaped through the crack. By nighttime, it was dark again.

135044—180 Days of Rea...

Authors

Kristi Sturgeon, M.Ed.

Heather Schwartz

Program Credits

Corinne Burton, M.A.Ed., *President* and *Publisher*
Emily R. Smith, M.A.Ed., *SVP of Content Development*
Véronique Bos, *Vice President of Creative*
Lynette Ordoñez, *Content Manager*
Ashley Oberhaus, M.Ed., *Content Specialist*
Melissa Laughlin, *Editor*
David Slayton, *Assistant Editor*
Jill Malcolm, *Graphic Designer*

Image Credits: p.104 Shutterstock/Grindstone Media Group; p.119 Shutterstock/elinba; p.158 Jill Malcolm; p.173 NASA pp.176 NASA; p.209 iStock/gnagel; p.211 Shutterstock/Gino Santa Maria; p.212 Wikimedia/Library of Congress; p.218 Library of Congress [LC-USZC4-6147]; all other images Shutterstock and/or iStock

Standards

A division of Teacher Created Materials
5482 Argosy Avenue
Huntington Beach, CA 92649
www.tcmpub.com/shell-education
ISBN 979-8-7659-1804-3
© 2024 Shell Educational Publishing, Inc.
Printed in China 51497

Table of Contents

Introduction

The Need for Practice

To be successful in today's reading classroom, students must deeply understand both concepts and procedures so that they can discuss and demonstrate their understanding. Demonstrating understanding is a process that must be continually practiced for students to be successful. According to Robert Marzano, "Practice has always been, and always will be, a necessary ingredient to learning procedural knowledge at a level at which students execute it independently" (2010, 83). Practice is especially important to help students apply reading comprehension strategies and word-study skills. *180 Days of Reading* offers teachers and parents a full page of reading comprehension and word recognition practice activities for each day of the school year.

The Science of Reading

For some people, reading comes easily. They barely remember how it happened. For others, learning to read takes more effort.

The goal of reading research is to understand the differences in how people learn to read and find the best ways to help all students learn. The term *Science of Reading* is commonly used to refer to this body of research. It helps people understand how to provide instruction in learning the code of the English language, how to develop fluency, and how to navigate challenging text and make sense of it.

Much of this research has been around for decades. In fact, in the late 1990s, Congress commissioned a review of the reading research. In 2000, the National Reading Panel (NRP) published a report that became the backbone of the Science of Reading. The NRP report highlights five components of effective reading instruction. These include the following:

- **Phonemic Awareness:** understanding and manipulating individual speech sounds
- **Phonics:** matching sounds to letters for use in reading and spelling
- **Fluency:** reading connected text accurately and smoothly
- **Vocabulary:** knowing the meanings of words in speech and in print
- **Reading Comprehension:** understanding what is read

There are two commonly referenced frameworks that build on reading research and provide a visual way for people to understand what is needed to learn to read. In the mid-1980s, a framework called the Simple View of Reading was introduced (Gough and Tunmer 1986). It shows that reading comprehension is possible when students are able to decode (or read) the words and have the language to understand the words.

The Simple View of Reading

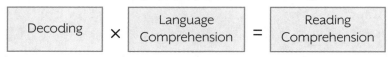

Another framework that builds on the research behind the Science of Reading is Scarborough's Reading Rope (Scarborough 2001). It shows specific skills needed for both language comprehension and word recognition. The "strands" of the rope for language comprehension include having background content knowledge, knowing vocabulary, understanding language structure, having verbal reasoning, and understanding literacy. Word recognition includes phonological awareness, decoding skills, and sight recognition of familiar words (Scarborough 2001). As individual skills are strengthened and practiced, they become increasingly strategic and automatic to promote reading comprehension.

The Science of Reading (cont.)

Many parts of our understanding of how people learn to read stand the test of time and have been confirmed by more recent studies. However, new research continues to add to the understanding of reading. Some of this research shows the importance of wide reading (reading about a variety of topics), motivation, and self-regulation. The conversation will never be over, as new research will continue to refine the understanding of how people learn to read. There is always more to learn!

180 Days of Reading has been informed by this reading research. This series provides opportunities for students to practice the skills that years of research indicate contribute to reading growth. There are several features in this book that are supported by the Science of Reading.

Text Selection

- Carefully chosen texts offer experiences in a **wide range of text types**. Each unit includes nonfiction, fiction, and a nontraditional text type or genre (e.g., letters, newspaper articles, advertisements, menus).

- Texts intentionally build upon one another to help students **build background knowledge** from day to day.

- Engaging with texts on the same topic for a thematic unit enables students to become familiar with related **vocabulary**, **language structure**, and **literacy knowledge**. This allows reading to become increasingly strategic and automatic, leading to better **fluency** and **comprehension**.

Activity Design

- Specific **language comprehension** and **word-recognition skills** are reinforced throughout the activities.

- Each text includes a purpose for reading and an opportunity to practice various reading strategies through annotation. This promotes **close reading** of the text.

- Paired fiction and nonfiction texts are used to promote **comparison** and encourage students to **make connections** between texts within a unit.

- Students **write to demonstrate understanding** of the texts. Students provide written responses in a variety of forms, including short answers, open-ended responses, and creating their own versions of nontraditional texts.

This book provides the regular practice of reading skills that students need as they develop into excellent readers.

How to Use This Resource

Unit Structure Overview

This resource is organized into twelve units. Each three-week unit follows a consistent format for ease of use.

Week 1: Nonfiction

Day 1	Students read nonfiction and answer multiple-choice questions.
Day 2	Students read nonfiction and answer multiple-choice questions.
Day 3	Students read nonfiction and answer multiple-choice, short-answer, and open-response questions.
Day 4	Students read a longer nonfictional text, answer multiple-choice questions, and complete graphic organizers.
Day 5	Students reread the text from Day 4 and answer reading-response questions.

Week 2: Fiction

Day 1	Students read fiction and answer multiple-choice questions.
Day 2	Students read fiction and answer multiple-choice questions.
Day 3	Students read fiction and answer multiple-choice, short-answer, and open-response questions.
Day 4	Students read a longer fictional text, answer multiple-choice questions, and complete graphic organizers.
Day 5	Students reread the text from Day 4 and answer reading-response questions.

Week 3: Nontraditional Text

Day 1	Students read nontraditional text and answer multiple-choice and open-response questions.
Day 2	Students complete close-reading activities with paired texts from the unit.
Day 3	Students complete close-reading activities with paired texts from the unit.
Day 4	Students create their own nontraditional texts.
Day 5	Students write their own versions of the nontraditional text from Day 1.

How to Use This Resource (cont.)

Unit Structure Overview (cont.)

Paired Texts

State standards have brought into focus the importance of preparing students for college and career success by expanding their critical-thinking and analytical skills. It is no longer enough for students to read and comprehend a single text on a topic. Rather, the integration of ideas across texts is crucial for a more comprehensive understanding of themes presented by authors.

Literacy specialist Jennifer Soalt has written that paired texts are "uniquely suited to scaffolding and extending students' comprehension" (2005, 680). She identifies three ways in which paired fiction and nonfiction are particularly effective in increasing comprehension: the building of background knowledge, the development of vocabulary, and the increase in student motivation (Soalt 2005).

Each three-week unit in *180 Days of Reading* is connected by a common theme or topic. Packets of each week's or each unit's practice pages can be prepared for students.

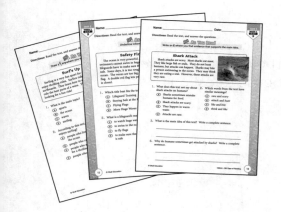

During Week 1, students read nonfictional texts and answer questions.

During Week 2, students read fictional texts and answer questions.

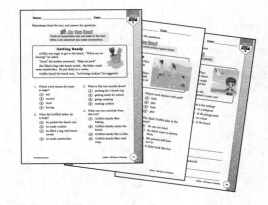

During Week 3, students read nontraditional texts (advertisements, poems, letters, etc.), answer questions, and complete close-reading and writing activities.

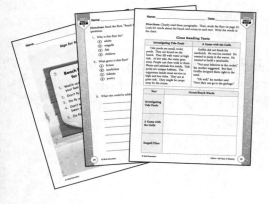

How to Use This Resource *(cont.)*

Student Practice Pages

Practice pages reinforce grade-level skills across a variety of reading concepts for each day of the school year. Each day's reading activity is provided as a full practice page, making them easy to prepare and implement as part of a morning routine, at the beginning of each reading lesson, or as homework.

Practice Pages for Weeks 1 and 2

Days 1 and 2 of each week follow a consistent format, with a short text passage and multiple-choice questions.

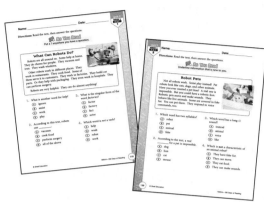

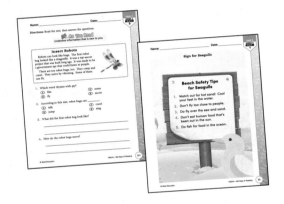

Days 3 and 4 have a combination of multiple-choice, short-answer, and open-response questions.

On day 5, students complete text-based writing prompts.

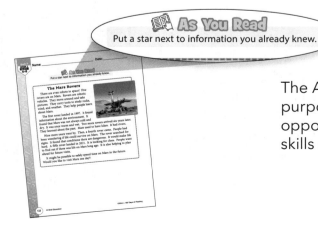

The As You Read activities give students a purpose for reading the texts and provide opportunities to practice various reading skills and strategies.

How to Use This Resource *(cont.)*

Student Practice Pages *(cont.)*

Practice Pages for Week 3

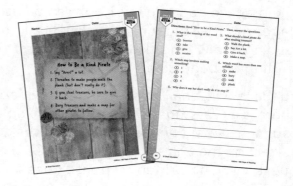

Day 1 of this week follows a consistent format, with a nontraditional text and multiple-choice and open-response questions.

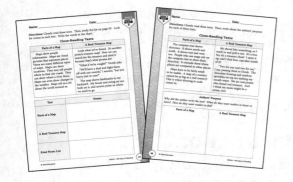

On days 2 and 3, students engage in close-reading activities of paired texts. Students are encouraged to compare and contrast different aspects of the texts they read throughout the unit.

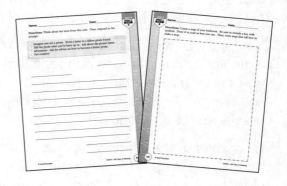

On days 4 and 5, students think about the texts in the unit, respond to a writing prompt, and construct their own versions of diverse texts. Students are encouraged to use information from texts throughout the unit to inspire and support their writing.

Instructional Options

180 Days of Reading is a flexible resource that can be used in various instructional settings for different purposes.

- Use these student pages as daily warm-up activities or as review.

- Work with students in small groups, allowing them to focus on specific skills. This setting also lends itself to partner and group discussions about the texts.

- Student pages in this resource can be completed independently during center times and as activities for early finishers.

How to Use This Resource (cont.)

Diagnostic Assessment

The practice pages in this book can be used as diagnostic assessments. These activity pages require students to think critically, respond to text-dependent questions, and utilize reading and writing skills and strategies. (An answer key for the practice pages is provided starting on page 230.)

For each unit, analysis sheets are provided as *Microsoft Word®* files in the digital resources. There is a *Class Analysis Sheet* and an *Individual Analysis Sheet*. Use the file that matches your assessment needs. After each week, record how many answers each student got correct on the unit's analysis sheet. Only record the answers for the multiple-choice questions. The written-response questions and graphic organizers can be evaluated using the writing rubric or other evaluation tools (see below). At the end of each unit, analyze the data on the analysis sheet to determine instructional focuses for your child or class.

The diagnostic analysis tools included in the digital resources allow for quick evaluation and ongoing monitoring of student work. See at a glance which reading genre students may need to focus on further to develop proficiency.

Using the Results to Differentiate Instruction

Once results are gathered and analyzed, use the data to inform the way to differentiate instruction. The data can help determine which concepts are the most difficult for students and that need additional instructional support and continued practice.

The results of the diagnostic analysis may show that an entire class is struggling with a particular genre. If these concepts have been taught in the past, this indicates that further instruction or reteaching is necessary. If these concepts have not been taught yet, this data is a great preassessment and demonstrates that students do not have a working knowledge of the concepts.

The results of the diagnostic analysis may also show that an individual or small group of students is struggling with a particular concept or group of concepts. Consider pulling aside these students while others are working independently to instruct further on the concept(s). You can also use the results to help identify individuals or groups of proficient students who are ready for enrichment or above-grade-level instruction. These students may benefit from independent learning contracts or more challenging activities.

Writing Rubric

A rubric for written responses is provided on page 229. Display the rubric for students to reference as they write. Score students' written responses, and provide them with feedback on their writing.

Name: _____   Date: _____

Directions: Read the text, and answer the questions.

 **As You Read**

Draw a ♀ anywhere you have questions or want to know more.

Surf's Up

Surfing is a very fun sport for people who enjoy thrilling rides. Surfers ride waves on their surfboards. They learn how to stand up. They ride the best parts of a wave. They are always looking for a fun ride!

1. What is the main topic?
- Ⓐ sports
- Ⓑ the ocean
- Ⓒ waves
- Ⓓ surfing

2. According to this text, who enjoys surfing?
- Ⓐ people who live near the ocean
- Ⓑ people who can swim
- Ⓒ people who are looking for a thrilling ride
- Ⓓ people who can stand up

3. Which of these words from the text is a compound word?
- Ⓐ thrilling
- Ⓑ looking
- Ⓒ surfboards
- Ⓓ surfers

4. What does the word *thrilling* mean?
- Ⓐ very exciting
- Ⓑ wet
- Ⓒ very scary
- Ⓓ water

Name: _____ Date: _____

Directions: Read the text, and answer the questions.

 **As You Read**

Underline information that is new or interesting to you.

Safety First

The ocean is very powerful. Even the strongest swimmers cannot swim in huge waves. So, lifeguards have to make sure that beaches are safe. Some days, it is too rough to swim in the ocean. The waves are too big. Lifeguards fly a flag. A double red flag lets people know the beach is closed.

1. Which new title best fits the text?
   - (A) Lifeguard Training
   - (B) Staying Safe at the Beach
   - (C) Flying Flags
   - (D) More Huge Waves

2. What is a lifeguard's main job?
   - (A) to watch huge waves
   - (B) to swim in the ocean
   - (C) to fly flags at the beach
   - (D) to make sure the beach is safe

3. What is the root word in *powerful*?
   - (A) owe
   - (B) power
   - (C) wer
   - (D) ful

4. Which of these things might be considered too rough?
   - (A) sitting on a bed
   - (B) swinging high on the swings
   - (C) a hard push in a game of tag
   - (D) a soccer goal

135044—180 Days of Reading

Name: _____ **Date:** _____

Directions: Read the text, and answer the questions.

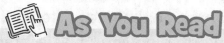 As You Read

Draw a ☆ next to information you think is important.

Shark Attack

Shark attacks are scary. Most sharks eat meat. They like large fish or seals. They do not hunt humans, but attacks can happen. Sharks may bite a person swimming in the ocean. They may think they are eating a seal. However, these attacks are very rare.

1. What does this text **not** say about shark attacks on humans?

   Ⓐ Sharks sometimes mistake humans for food.

   Ⓑ Shark attacks are scary.

   Ⓒ They happen in warm water.

   Ⓓ Attacks are rare.

2. Which words from the text have similar meanings?

   Ⓐ *rare* and *scary*

   Ⓑ *attack* and *hunt*

   Ⓒ *like* and *bite*

   Ⓓ *think* and *like*

3. What is the main idea of this text?

_____

_____

4. Why do humans sometimes get attacked by sharks?

_____

_____

As You Read
Underline information that is new to you. Draw
a ☆ next to information you think is interesting.

Investigating Tide Pools

Tide pools are small, rocky pools. They are found on beaches. They fill with water at high tide. At low tide, the water goes away. People can then walk to them. Plants and animals live inside them.

Tide pools are unique habitats. The organisms inside must survive in high and low tides. They are at great risk. They might be swept away by the ocean. Or seagulls could snack on them. Too much sun can dry them out, too.

Sea stars live in tide pools. Sea stars come in a variety of sizes and colors. They like to eat mussels. A sea star wants to eat a mussel before a seagull eats it instead!

Anemones (uh-NEH-muh-neez) also live in tide pools. They eat very tiny fish. Anemones are fun to spot. They look a bit like flowers. They add a lot of color to tide pools.

Directions: Read "Investigating Tide Pools." Then, answer the questions.

1. Which shows a strong connection to the text?
   - (A) I like to play in the sandbox at the park.
   - (B) I play at the beach with my grandparents.
   - (C) I noticed a tide pool on the beach and studied the creatures inside.
   - (D) A sea star is a star.

2. When does the water leave the tide pool?
   - (A) at high tide
   - (B) at low tide
   - (C) at sunset
   - (D) at sunrise

3. Why is a tide pool a unique habitat?
   - (A) Sea stars all look the same.
   - (B) Birds prey on the food there.
   - (C) It survives in low and high tides.
   - (D) It is found on the beach.

4. Which is the best summary of the text?
   - (A) Tide pools are unique habitats with interesting plants and animals.
   - (B) Sea stars like to eat mussels.
   - (C) Tide pools take up space on our beaches.
   - (D) Anemones eat tiny fish.

5. Use details from the text to draw and write about each type of tide pool.

Low tide tide pool	
High tide tide pool	

Name: _____ **Date:** _____

Directions: Reread "Investigating Tide Pools." Then, respond to the prompt.

Think about what you would want to see on a trip to the beach. Write about which creatures you would look for when you walk along the sand. Then, draw a picture of it.

_____

_____

_____

_____

_____

Directions: Read the text, and answer the questions.

 **As You Read**

Think of connections you can make to the text.
Write a ∞ whenever you make connections.

Getting Ready

Griffin was eager to get to the beach. "When are we leaving?" he asked.

"Soon," his mother answered. "Help me pack." She filled a bag with beach towels.

His father made some sandwiches. He put them in a cooler.

Griffin found the beach toys. "Let's bring cookies," he suggested.

1. Which word means the same as *eager*?
   - Ⓐ sad
   - Ⓑ excited
   - Ⓒ tired
   - Ⓓ boring

2. What does Griffin's father do to help?
   - Ⓐ He packs the beach toys.
   - Ⓑ He makes cookies.
   - Ⓒ He fills a bag with beach towels.
   - Ⓓ He makes sandwiches.

3. What is this text mostly about?
   - Ⓐ packing for a beach trip
   - Ⓑ getting ready for school
   - Ⓒ going camping
   - Ⓓ making cookies

4. Which is a strong conclusion from this text?
   - Ⓐ Griffin's family likes baking.
   - Ⓑ Griffin's family enjoys the beach.
   - Ⓒ Griffin's family likes to hike.
   - Ⓓ Griffin's family likes road trips.

Name: _____ Date: _____

Directions: Read the text, and answer the questions.

As You Read

Draw an 👁 next to words that help you visualize the story.

Caring for the Dunes

The dunes looked like mountains. They were made of sand. What a fun place to play!

But Griffin did not want to destroy them. The family kept walking. They took a path to the beach. They found a better spot to sit and play.

1. What are dunes made from?

   (A) dirt

   (B) mud

   (C) sand

   (D) water

2. What does the family do after seeing the dunes?

   (A) plays in them

   (B) keeps walking

   (C) takes pictures

   (D) sits down

3. Which word rhymes with *path*?

   (A) bath

   (B) play

   (C) both

   (D) plot

4. Why doesn't Griffin play in the dunes?

   (A) He is too tired.

   (B) He doesn't want to destroy them.

   (C) His parents tell him not to.

   (D) It doesn't look like fun.

Directions: Read the text, and answer the questions.

As You Read
Draw a ♡ next to your favorite part(s).

A Seagull Shows Up

Griffin's family sat on a blanket together. They looked at the ocean. Big waves crashed on the shore.

Griffin was not ready to swim. He was not ready to play. His stomach grumbled. He unwrapped his sandwich and took a bite. Yum!

Suddenly, a seagull swooped down from the sky. Griffin was startled. He laughed. The bird wanted a taste, too!

1. What can you infer from the following text?
   His stomach grumbled. He unwrapped his sandwich and took a bite. Yum!
   - Ⓐ Griffin feels sick.
   - Ⓑ Griffin is hungry.
   - Ⓒ Griffin is upset.
   - Ⓓ Griffin is frustrated.

2. What is the setting?
   - Ⓐ in a tide pool
   - Ⓑ at the playground
   - Ⓒ in a boat
   - Ⓓ at the beach

3. Tell why Griffin is not ready to swim.

   _____

   _____

4. How would you feel if a seagull ate your sandwich?

   _____

   _____

Name: _____   Date: _____

 **As You Read**

Write an **S** whenever you identify a part of the setting.

A Game with the Gulls

Griffin did not finish his sandwich. He was too excited. He wanted to jump in the waves and build a sandcastle.

"Put your leftovers in the cooler," his mother suggested. But then Griffin dropped them right in the sand.

"Oh well," his mother said. "Now they can go in the garbage."

Griffin went over to the garbage can. It was stuffed. He set his trash on the very top and started to walk away.

"Look!" his father called out, pointing.

Griffin turned around just in time to see. A seagull was on the garbage can. It poked at the trash. It pulled out a bag and flew away with it. The gull landed on the sand. It pulled napkins and food wrappers out of the bag. Griffin laughed. Then he realized what was happening.

"Stop that!" Griffin cried. "You're making a big mess!"

Napkins flew through the air. Food wrappers blew across the beach. Griffin raced after them. His parents chased them, too. The wind tried to take the trash away. Other seagulls circled overhead. They wanted the trash, too. It was like a game.

His mother snatched up an empty cup. His father got a paper plate. Griffin grabbed a candy wrapper.

"Got it!" he yelled.

His family was faster than the gulls. They cleaned up all the trash.

"We won!" Griffin said. Next time, he would be more careful. Gulls should not play with garbage!

Directions: Read "A Game with the Gulls." Then, answer the questions.

1. Which two words from the story have the same meaning?
   - (A) *fast* and *careful*
   - (B) *garbage* and *trash*
   - (C) *yelled* and *laughed*
   - (D) *stuffed* and *empty*

2. Who snatches up an empty cup?
   - (A) Mother
   - (B) Father
   - (C) Griffin
   - (D) all of them

3. Which is a compound word?
   - (A) garbage
   - (B) napkin
   - (C) sandcastle
   - (D) wrapper

4. What does Griffin want to do at the beach?
   - (A) chase birds
   - (B) build a sandcastle
   - (C) swim with his parents
   - (D) fly a kite

5. Write five nouns and five verbs from the text.

Nouns	Verbs

Name: _____ **Date:** _____

Directions: Reread "A Game with the Gulls." Then, respond to the prompt.

What if Griffin did not set his trash on top of the trash can? Write a new ending. Tell what he did differently. Tell what else happened in the story.

Griffin went over to the garbage can. It was stuffed. _____

_____

_____

_____

_____

_____

_____

_____

_____

_____

_____

_____

Beach Safety Tips
for Seagulls

1. Watch out for hot sand! Cool your feet in the water.

2. **Don't** fly too close to people.

3. **Do** fly over the sea and sand.

4. **Don't** eat human food that's been out in the sun.

5. **Do** fish for food in the ocean.

Name: _____ **Date:** _____

Directions: Read the flyer, "Beach Safety Tips for Seagulls." Then, answer the questions.

1. Who is this flyer for?
   - (A) adults
   - (B) seagulls
   - (C) fish
   - (D) children

2. What genre is this flyer?
   - (A) fiction
   - (B) nonfiction
   - (C) folktale
   - (D) poetry

3. Why does the flyer suggest putting feet in the water?
   - (A) to splash people
   - (B) to clean them
   - (C) to cool them off
   - (D) to test the water temperature

4. What is the purpose of this flyer?
   - (A) to keep the beach clean
   - (B) to keep seagulls safe
   - (C) to warn humans about seagulls
   - (D) to teach about the ocean

5. What else could be added to this flyer? Write a few ideas.

   _____

   _____

   _____

   _____

   _____

   _____

Directions: Closely read these texts. Then, study the flyer on page 23. Underline words about the beach and ocean in each text. Write the words in the chart.

Close-Reading Texts

Investigating Tide Pools	A Game with the Gulls
Tide pools are small, rocky pools. They are found on the beach. They fill with water at high tide. At low tide, the water goes away. People can then walk to them. Plants and animals live inside. Tide pools are unique habitats. The organisms inside must survive in high and low tides. They are at great risk. They might be swept away by the ocean.	Griffin did not finish his sandwich. He was too excited. He wanted to jump in the waves. He wanted to build a sandcastle. "Put your leftovers in the cooler," his mother suggested. But then Griffin dropped them right in the sand. "Oh well," his mother said. "Now they can go in the garbage."

Text	Ocean/Beach Words
Investigating Tide Pools	
A Game with the Gulls	
Seagull Flyer	

Name: _____ **Date:** _____

Directions: Closely read these texts. Then, write about the authors' purpose for each of these texts.

Close-Reading Texts

Investigating Tide Pools	A Game with the Gulls
Sea stars live in tide pools. Sea stars come in a variety of sizes and colors. They like to eat mussels. A sea star wants to eat a mussel before a seagull eats it instead! Anemones (uh-NEH-muh-neez) also live in tide pools. They eat very tiny fish. Anemones are fun to spot. They look a bit like flowers.	"Stop that!" Griffin cried. "You're making a big mess!" Napkins flew through the air. Food wrappers blew across the beach. Griffin raced after them. His parents chased them, too. The wind tried to take the trash away. Other seagulls circled overhead. They wanted the trash, too. It was like a game.

Authors' Purpose

Why did the author write the text? What do they want readers to know or learn? How do they want readers to feel?

Investigating Tide Pools	A Game with the Gulls
_____	_____
_____	_____
_____	_____
_____	_____
_____	_____
_____	_____

Name: _____ **Date:** _____

Directions: Think about the texts from this unit. Then, respond to the prompt.

Your family is planning a trip to the beach. What will you bring? What people in your family will be going? What events happen once you get there? Use details to tell a story about your beach trip.

_____

_____

_____

_____

_____

_____

_____

_____

_____

_____

_____

Name: _____ **Date:** _____

Directions: Design a flyer to be posted at the beach. This time, it is intended for people. Be sure to give details about what people should and should not do while at the beach.

Directions: Read the text, and answer the questions.

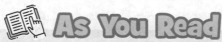 **As You Read**

Draw a rectangle around new or important vocabulary words.

Dinosaurs

Dinosaurs used to roam Earth. Now they are gone. We do not know for sure where they went or what happened to them. Scientists have theories. Some say an asteroid hit Earth, while others think a disease spread among the dinosaurs. An ice age may have started it all. We may never know the whole truth.

1. What is the main idea of this text?

   (A) Scientists develop theories.

   (B) The reason why dinosaurs are gone is a mystery.

   (C) Asteroids hit Earth.

   (D) An ice age may have happened.

2. Which idea is **not** suggested as a reason why dinosaurs are gone?

   (A) disease

   (B) asteroids

   (C) an ice age

   (D) a volcano erupting

3. What is the root word in *started*?

   (A) tart

   (B) start

   (C) ted

   (D) art

4. Which word is a synonym for *roam*?

   (A) destroy

   (B) attack

   (C) rule

   (D) travel

Name: _____ Date: _____

Directions: Read the text, and answer the questions.

Underline information that is new to you.

Sea Turtle Trouble

Sea turtles are amazing. They can swim a long way. They can swim over 1,000 miles (1,609 kilometers)! But sea turtles are in trouble. Their numbers are low. Their nests are disturbed by humans. People take their eggs. The babies cannot survive. This is a big problem.

1. Which new title best fits the text?

- (A) Nest Disturbance
- (B) A Long Swim
- (C) Sea Turtles in Danger
- (D) All About Baby Turtles

2. What is the problem?

- (A) Sea turtles swim a long way.
- (B) Sea turtles' nests and eggs are disturbed.
- (C) Sea turtles get tired when they cross oceans.
- (D) Sea turtles are amazing ocean animals.

3. How many syllables are in the word *survive*?

- (A) one syllable
- (B) two syllables
- (C) three syllables
- (D) four syllables

4. What does the phrase *numbers are low* mean in the text?

- (A) Sea turtles are swimming lower.
- (B) The sea turtles are eating less.
- (C) Sea turtles are getting smaller.
- (D) The number of sea turtles is shrinking.

Directions: Read the text, and answer the questions.

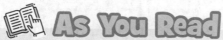 As You Read

Place a **?** anywhere you have a question or would like more information.

The Power of Plants

Plants can become extinct. When they are extinct, they are gone forever. One fewer species might not seem like a big deal. There are many others left. But plants are vital to life. People need plants to stay alive. Other living things depend on plants, too.

1. Which word has the same root word as *living*?
   - (A) having
   - (B) lived
   - (C) loving
   - (D) olive

2. Which two words are synonyms?
   - (A) *plant* and *thing*
   - (B) *animal* and *vital*
   - (C) *alive* and *living*
   - (D) *extinct* and *less*

3. What is the main idea of this text?

   _____

   _____

4. Do you think people should worry about plants becoming extinct? Why or why not?

   _____

   _____

   _____

Name: _____ Date: _____

 **As You Read**

Put a ☆ next to important information.

Ecosystems

Our world has many creatures. We all depend on one another. We need one another to survive. One creature may die out. That changes the rest of the living world.

For example, imagine a lake full of fish. Humans want them for food. So, they fish for them. Over time, there are fewer fish. But the fish are part of a large ecosystem. They eat tadpoles. They eat insects. With fewer fish, there are now more insects. There are many more frogs, and the frogs need more food. Frogs eat dragonflies. But now they have eaten too many dragonflies. The ecosystem has changed. Humans caused this problem. The fish in the lake are almost gone.

What can humans do now? How can they fix the problem? Some people may suggest closing the lake. Perhaps there will be no fishing there for several years. This would give the fish time to come back. It would help restore the balance of life in that lake. These kinds of problems are happening in many places. Many animals face this kind of issue. Humans are often the problem. But they can be part of the solution, too.

Directions: Read "Ecosystems." Then, answer the questions.

1. Which experience would help you understand the text better?
   - (A) Yesterday, I noticed there were a lot of insects around.
   - (B) I have tasted fish before, and I don't like it.
   - (C) My sister and I swim in the lake on the weekends.
   - (D) The local pond is closed for the winter because the water is too cold.

2. Which best summarizes the text?
   - (A) All living creatures eat tadpoles.
   - (B) Living creatures depend on one another for a healthy ecosystem.
   - (C) All living creatures need clean lakes as a habitat.
   - (D) A lake needs more fish.

3. Which animals are **not** mentioned in the text?
   - (A) fish
   - (B) tadpoles
   - (C) insects
   - (D) snakes

4. What is the problem?
   - (A) hungry frogs
   - (B) a destroyed ecosystem
   - (C) a lack of fish for fishermen
   - (D) a cold lake

5. Write three new facts you learned about ecosystems.

Fact 1	
Fact 2	
Fact 3	

Name: _____ **Date:** _____

Directions: Reread "Ecosystems." Then, respond to the prompt.

Think about how everything that is alive is connected.

Write about what this reminds you of in your own life. Draw a picture to go with your writing.

_____

_____

_____

_____

_____

_____

Name: _____ Date: _____

Directions: Read the text, and answer the questions.

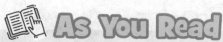

Think of connections you can make to the text.
Write a ∞ whenever you make connections.

I Am a Superhero!

I love all kinds of animals. Foxes are my favorite. I love bears and tigers, too. Some wild animals are endangered. They could become extinct. This means there will be no more of them. They will all be gone. I worry about this. Someone should do something to help. I am a superhero! I have a secret superpower. I can save these animals!

1. What is the meaning of *extinct*?
   - A) smelly
   - B) gone forever
   - C) super
   - D) only a few

2. Which animal is the narrator's favorite?
   - A) foxes
   - B) elephants
   - C) tigers
   - D) bears

3. Why is the narrator worried?
   - A) The narrator is scared of tigers.
   - B) The narrator does not like being a superhero.
   - C) The narrator is afraid more animals will become extinct.
   - D) The narrator fears heights.

4. Which word from the text is a compound word?
   - A) animal
   - B) secret
   - C) extinct
   - D) superhero

Name: _____   Date: _____

Directions: Read the text, and answer the questions.

Write an **N** wherever you read the narrator's opinion.

I Can Save Plants, Too!

Some plants are also endangered. Certain flowers could be lost forever. Trees could be lost, too. This is terrible. I love all kinds of plants! I will not let this happen. My superpowers can help. I will protect plants. I will save them from extinction.

1. How does the narrator want to help?
   - (A) by using superpowers to protect plants
   - (B) by flying to see plants
   - (C) by watering the plants
   - (D) by creating new types of plants

2. What does the word *endangered* mean?
   - (A) gone
   - (B) lonely
   - (C) scared
   - (D) at risk

3. Which two words are synonyms?
   - (A) *lost* and *found*
   - (B) *help* and *assist*
   - (C) *terrible* and *wonderful*
   - (D) *save* and *destroy*

4. Which word has two syllables?
   - (A) plants
   - (B) protect
   - (C) forever
   - (D) extinction

Directions: Read the text, and answer the questions.

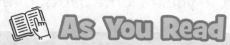 As You Read

Write an **S** whenever you identify a part of the setting.

Superhero at Work

I need more information. So, I go to the library. I want to find books on endangered plants and animals. I find them on the shelves. I read a few of them. I write notes on what I learn. Everyone thinks I am just a regular kid. No one knows I am a superhero. I am doing important superhero work.

1. Where does the narrator go for more information?

   Ⓐ superhero school

   Ⓑ the zoo

   Ⓒ library

   Ⓓ plant store

2. What does the narrator do *before* she writes things down?

   Ⓐ reads some books

   Ⓑ gets her glasses

   Ⓒ does superhero work

   Ⓓ has a snack

3. Explain what important superhero work the narrator is doing.

   _____

   _____

4. Where would you look if you wanted to learn more about endangered plants and animals?

   _____

   _____

As You Read

Put a ♡ next to your favorite part(s) of the story.

My Secret Is Out

My teacher, Mrs. Kanner, takes our class on a walk in the woods. "What do you think we'll see?" she asks.

Students raise their hands. Sophie guesses, "We'll see trees."

Advik says, "I bet we'll see flowers."

I raise my hand and ask, "Will we see endangered plants and animals?"

"We might," Mrs. Kanner answers with a smile.

This is my chance to save them! I close my eyes and imagine my invisible superhero cape. I see myself putting it on. OK, I'm ready to go!

As we walk on a path through the trees, I remember things I learned in the library. Will I see an eastern tiger salamander or a peregrine falcon? I hope so. They're endangered, and I want to help them. But how? Suddenly, I'm not so sure I can.

"Look at that pretty flower!" Sophie says. When I turn around, I see I have a job to do!

"Don't pick it!" I warn her. "It's a small white lady's slipper. It's endangered."

Mrs. Kanner hurries over to see. "You're right!" she tells me, sounding surprised.

Then, Advik calls out, "Look, a butterfly!"

My classmates run after it, but I don't. I can see that it's blue.

"Stop!" I shout. "That's a Karner blue butterfly! We can't catch it. It's endangered!"

Everyone stops running, and I feel happy and proud.

"You protected two endangered species," Mrs. Kanner says. "You must be some kind of superhero!"

Looks like my secret is out!

135044—180 Days of Reading   © Shell Education

Directions: Read "My Secret Is Out." Then, answer the questions.

1. What does the narrator imagine putting on?
   - (A) a robe
   - (B) an invisible cape
   - (C) spy glasses
   - (D) imaginary slippers

2. What is the name of the endangered flower in the text?
   - (A) eastern tiger salamander
   - (B) peregrine falcon
   - (C) white lady's slipper
   - (D) Karner blue butterfly

3. How many endangered species does the narrator protect?
   - (A) one
   - (B) two
   - (C) three
   - (D) four

4. Why does the narrator yell *stop* when the classmates chase the butterfly?
   - (A) The narrator wants to catch up to them.
   - (B) The narrator likes to be loud.
   - (C) The narrator doesn't want them to harm it.
   - (D) The narrator wants a chance to catch it.

5. Describe the beginning, middle, and end of the story.

Beginning	Middle	End

Directions: Reread "My Secret Is Out." Then, respond to the prompt.

Imagine you are on a walk in the woods. What are you hoping to see? What will you do if you come across an endangered plant or animal? Describe your walk. Draw a picture of what you see.

_____

_____

_____

_____

_____

_____

Save the Sea Turtles!

Building sandcastles on the beach? Be sure to knock them down before you go. Sandcastles can get in the way when turtles need to nest!

Name: _____ **Date:** _____

Directions: Read the poster titled, "Save the Sea Turtles!" Then, answer the questions.

1. Which animal does this poster help protect?

   (A) sand crabs

   (B) sea turtles

   (C) sea stars

   (D) fish

2. Which word from the text is a compound word?

   (A) building

   (B) before

   (C) sandcastle

   (D) turtle

3. What is the root word in *building*?

   (A) build

   (B) ing

   (C) buy

   (D) make

4. What does it mean for sea turtles to *nest*?

   (A) lay eggs in the sand

   (B) make a nest for a bird

   (C) swim underwater

   (D) feed their babies

5. You see kids at the beach making a sandcastle. What can you say to them so they help sea turtles?

   _____

   _____

   _____

Name: _____ **Date:** _____

Directions: Closely read these texts. Then, study the poster on page 41. Look for action verbs in each text. Write the words in the chart.

Close-Reading Texts

Ecosystems	My Secret Is Out
Our world has many creatures. We all depend on one another. We need one another to survive. One creature may die out. That changes the rest of the living world. For example, imagine a lake full of fish. Humans want them for food. So, they fish for them. Over time, there are fewer fish.	My teacher, Mrs. Kanner, takes our class on a walk in the woods. "What do you think we'll see?" she asks. Students raise their hands. Sophie guesses, "We'll see trees." Advik says, "I bet we'll see flowers." I raise my hand and ask, "Will we see endangered plants and animals?" "We might," Mrs. Kanner answers with a smile.

Text	Action Verbs
Ecosystems	
My Secret Is Out	
Sea Turtle Poster	

Name: _____ Date: _____

Directions: Closely read these texts. Then, write about the authors' purpose for each of these texts.

Close-Reading Texts

Ecosystems	My Secret Is Out
What can humans do now? How can they fix the problem? Some people may suggest closing the lake. Perhaps there will be no fishing there for several years. This would give the fish time to come back. It would help restore the balance of life in that lake. These kinds of problems are happening in many places. Many animals face this kind of issue. Humans are often the problem. But they can be the solution, too.	My classmates run after it, but not me. I can see that it's blue. "Stop!" I shout. "That's a Karner blue butterfly! We can't catch it. It's endangered!" Everyone stops running, and I feel happy and proud. "You protected two endangered species," Mrs. Kanner says. "You must be some kind of superhero!" Looks like my secret is out!

Authors' Purpose

Why did the author write the text? What do they want readers to know or learn? How do they want readers to feel?

Ecosystems	My Secret Is Out
_____	_____
_____	_____
_____	_____
_____	_____
_____	_____

Name: _____ **Date:**_____

Directions: Think about the texts from this unit. Then, respond to the prompt.

If you could have any superpower, what would it be? What problem would you want to solve? Describe how your superpower solves this problem. Draw a picture to show how you use your superpower.

_____

_____

_____

_____

_____

_____

_____

_____

_____

_____

_____

Name: _____ **Date:** _____

Directions: Create your own endangered plant or animal. Give it a name. Then, design a poster to educate others. Include the answers to these questions on your poster:

- What should people do if they see this plant or animal?
- How can a human be a part of the solution in protecting it?

Directions: Read the text, and answer the questions.

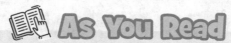 As You Read

Put a ☆ next to information you already knew.

Kitten Care

New pets need special care. Kittens need quality food made just for them. They need plenty of water. Kittens need to be brushed, too. This keeps their fur clean. Playing is also important. Kittens love to play! Then it's time to rest. Kittens might want to cuddle and sleep with their owners. They should have beds of their own, too.

1. What is the purpose of brushing a kitten?

   Ⓐ to keep its fur soft

   Ⓑ to keep its fur clean

   Ⓒ to get out tangles

   Ⓓ to practice brushing

2. What is the meaning of the word *quality* in the text?

   Ⓐ bad

   Ⓑ wet

   Ⓒ good

   Ⓓ dry

3. What is **not** mentioned in this text?

   Ⓐ Kittens like to cuddle.

   Ⓑ Kittens need lots of water to drink.

   Ⓒ Kittens love to play.

   Ⓓ Kittens can jump high.

4. Which two words have opposite meanings?

   Ⓐ *special* and *unique*

   Ⓑ *quality* and *nice*

   Ⓒ *play* and *rest*

   Ⓓ *clean* and *neat*

Directions: Read the text, and answer the questions.

Underline information that is new to you.

Keeping Fish Healthy and Happy

Fish have different needs from other pets. They need a tank that is large enough to live in. They need room to swim around. They need room to grow, too. A filtration system keeps their water clean. An air pump helps them breathe. Some fish need a heater to warm up their water. These items will help you take good care of your fish. They will help you keep them healthy and happy.

1. What do fish need to keep their tank water clean?
   - (A) a scrub brush
   - (B) a filtration system
   - (C) an air pump
   - (D) a heater

2. Which word from the text has two syllables?
   - (A) water
   - (B) watch
   - (C) swim
   - (D) breathe

3. How does an air pump help fish in a tank?
   - (A) It helps them find food.
   - (B) It cleans their tank.
   - (C) It gives them shelter.
   - (D) It helps them breathe.

4. Which word rhymes with *grow*?
   - (A) two
   - (B) know
   - (C) towel
   - (D) watch

Directions: Read the text, and answer the questions.

 **As You Read**

Put a rectangle around new or interesting vocabulary words.

Pets and Allergies

Do you sneeze around certain animals? Do you cough or wheeze? Many people are allergic to cats and dogs. They must stay away from them. Medicine can help. People who are allergic to cats and dogs might do better with a pet that doesn't have fur. Why not try a turtle, snake, or lizard?

1. What would **not** be helpful if you are allergic to a certain animal?

   Ⓐ taking allergy medicine

   Ⓑ staying away from that animal

   Ⓒ getting a different pet

   Ⓓ cuddling the animal often

2. Which two words from the text rhyme?

   Ⓐ *stay* and *away*

   Ⓑ *must* and *many*

   Ⓒ *animal* and *allergic*

   Ⓓ *better* and *turtle*

3. What pet would you like to have if you were allergic to cats and dogs? Why?

   _____

   _____

4. What other pets do not have fur?

   _____

   _____

Name: _____ Date: _____

 **As You Read**

Put an **!** next to information that surprises you.

The Right Pet for Your Home

It is wise to think about where you live when choosing a pet. Do you live on a farm? Do you live in a small apartment? How much indoor and outdoor space do you have for an animal? Some pets need a lot of room to run around. Others are comfortable in smaller areas.

You might feel crowded with a large dog in a small apartment. The dog might feel crowded, too! But a smaller dog could fit just fine. All dogs need to go outside. But you do not need a big yard or a farm for a dog. You can take walks around your neighborhood. You can visit a dog park. You just need to make the time to do it.

Cats can live happily in large or small homes. They need some space to run and play. They also like high places to perch and hide. And they do not need a large outdoor area. Many people keep cats indoors so they can stay safe.

Pets such as hamsters, gerbils, fish, and lizards can live almost anywhere. They do not need to go outside at all. Do you have room for a cage? Do you have space for a tank? That's all they need!

Directions: Read "The Right Pet for Your Home." Then, answer the questions.

1. Which word means the same as *wise*?

- Ⓐ confusing
- Ⓑ silly
- Ⓒ smart
- Ⓓ unwise

2. Which pet needs to go outside a lot?

- Ⓐ dog
- Ⓑ cat
- Ⓒ rabbit
- Ⓓ fish

3. Which animal likes high places to perch and hide?

- Ⓐ cat
- Ⓑ dog
- Ⓒ hamster
- Ⓓ lizard

4. What is the best solution to having a dog and no backyard?

- Ⓐ Move to a new house with a backyard.
- Ⓑ Take the dog for walks around the neighborhood.
- Ⓒ Put them in a kennel.
- Ⓓ Take them to school.

5. Use details from the text to compare the two pets.

Cats	Dogs

Both

Name: _____ **Date:** _____

Directions: Reread "The Right Pet for Your Home." Then, respond to the prompt.

If you could have any pet, what would it be? Write about its needs. How would you and your family help your pet have a happy and healthy life? Draw a picture to support your writing.

_____

_____

_____

_____

_____

135044—180 Days of Reading   © Shell Education

Name: _____ **Date:** _____

Directions: Read the text, and answer the questions.

 **As You Read**

Think of connections you can make to the text.
Write a ∞ whenever you make connections.

Trying to Talk

Parakeets can learn to talk. My family is trying to teach me. Over and over, they say, "Hello, hello." They use a singsong voice. Sometimes they say, "Hello, Violet." That is my name.

While they are out of the house, I practice my words. I try to sound like a person. But when the phone rings, I get distracted. I listen to the new noise.

1. What is this text about?
- Ⓐ a family learning a new language
- Ⓑ a parakeet learning to talk
- Ⓒ taking singing lessons
- Ⓓ getting distracted

2. What suffix can be added to the root word *listen* to make a new word?
- Ⓐ –es
- Ⓑ –ly
- Ⓒ –er
- Ⓓ –tion

3. What does the parakeet do when the family leaves?
- Ⓐ practice its words
- Ⓑ eat a lot of food
- Ⓒ fly around the house
- Ⓓ sleep

4. What distracts Violet while practicing?
- Ⓐ the radio
- Ⓑ the TV
- Ⓒ people talking
- Ⓓ the phone ringing

Name: _____ Date: _____

Directions: Read the text, and answer the questions.

 **As You Read**

Draw an 👁 next to words that help you visualize.

Parakeet Pastimes

I still cannot talk like a person. But I can do parakeet things! I chirp and I swing. I chew on my cuttlebone. It is good for me because it sharpens my beak. I spend a lot of time preening. This is how I groom myself. I will have clean, fluffy feathers when my family returns home.

1. What is the definition of *preening*?

   A to sing

   B to clean

   C to sleep

   D to eat

2. What can the parakeet **not** do?

   A chirp

   B swing

   C preen

   D talk

3. Which word from the text has the same vowel sound as *clean*?

   A beak

   B groom

   C chew

   D chirp

4. Which word is used to describe the parakeet's feathers?

   A soft

   B bright

   C fluffy

   D dirty

Name: _____ **Date:** _____

Directions: Read the text, and answer the questions.

 **As You Read**

Draw a rectangle around new or interesting words.

Fun with a Friend?

There's a small mirror in my cage that is safe for me to play with. I look at the reflection in the mirror and feel confused. Is that me, or is it another bird? I'm not sure! I bob my head from side to side. Either way, it feels like I have a friend.

1. Which could be a strong title for this text?

   (A) Silly Bird

   (B) Flying High

   (C) Parakeet for Sale

   (D) The Red Parakeet

2. Which sentence from the text tells the reader the parakeet likes having the mirror?

   (A) "There's a small mirror in my cage."

   (B) "I look at my reflection and feel confused."

   (C) "Either way, it feels like I have a friend."

   (D) "I bob my head from side to side."

3. Why does the parakeet feel confused?

   _____

   _____

4. Explain a connection you can make to this text.

   _____

   _____

 **As You Read**

Put a ♡ next to your favorite part(s) of the story.

My Funny Phone Prank

At last, my family is home again. Now I have people to play with! First, we shake hands, and I use my claws to grasp their fingers. Next, they turn on some music, and we dance together.

They make small paper toys for me, and I nibble on a little paper ball. Inside, I find a surprise. There's a treat in the center. I am having so much fun!

After I eat, they say, "Hello, hello." They use the singsong voice, and I know they hope I will say the word back to them. I make a sound and wonder if I got it right.

"Just a minute," the father of my family says. "I think I heard the phone ring."

He answers it by saying, "Hello?"

I make the sound again, and my family looks surprised. Then, they start to laugh.

"That wasn't the phone! That was Violet playing a prank!" they say. "What a smart and funny bird!"

Name: _____ **Date:** _____

Directions: Read "My Funny Phone Prank." Then, answer the questions.

1. What happens just after the family turns on music?

   Ⓐ They shake hands.

   Ⓑ They dance together.

   Ⓒ Violet plays with a paper toy.

   Ⓓ The family sings.

2. What is the meaning of the word *grasp*?

   Ⓐ hold

   Ⓑ breathe

   Ⓒ fly

   Ⓓ sing

3. What does the parakeet find in the center of the paper ball?

   Ⓐ more paper

   Ⓑ another toy

   Ⓒ a treat

   Ⓓ seeds

4. Which context clue lets the reader know they are having fun?

   Ⓐ "My family is home again."

   Ⓑ "Then, they start to laugh."

   Ⓒ "I make the sound again."

   Ⓓ "I make a sound and wonder."

5. List and describe the characters and the setting in the story.

Characters	
Setting	

Name: _____ **Date:** _____

Directions: Reread "My Funny Phone Prank." Then, respond to the prompt.

You are now the parakeet, the narrator of the story. What would you add or change about the prank? What might you or the family do differently? Retell the story with you as the parakeet.

_____

_____

_____

_____

_____

_____

_____

_____

_____

_____

_____

DOG WALKER WANTED

Seeking a reliable dog walker for my very friendly and well-behaved golden retriever. His name is Gunther. He needs to be walked once a day. He likes long walks and going to the dog park. Must be available Monday through Friday. Must love dogs. Great pay for a fun job!

Please call 555-342-8617.

Name: _____ **Date:** _____

Directions: Read "Dog Walker Wanted." Then, answer the questions.

1. How many times a day does Gunther need to be walked?

   (A) one time

   (B) two times

   (C) three times

   (D) none

2. What is the meaning of *reliable*?

   (A) outgoing

   (B) dependable

   (C) funny

   (D) honest

3. According to the ad, what does Gunther like to do?

   (A) swim

   (B) eat

   (C) sleep in

   (D) go on long walks

4. Which word from the ad has a suffix?

   (A) very

   (B) through

   (C) friendly

   (D) name

5. What other information could be added to this advertisement?

   _____

   _____

   _____

   _____

   _____

   _____

   _____

Name: _____ **Date:** _____

Directions: Closely read these texts. Then, study the ad on page 59. Look for nouns in each text. Write the words in the chart.

Close-Reading Texts

The Right Pet for Your Home	My Funny Phone Prank
It is wise to think about where you live when choosing a pet. Do you live on a farm? Do you live in a small apartment? How much indoor and outdoor space do you have for an animal? Some pets need a lot of room to run around. Others are comfortable in smaller areas.	At last, my family is home again. Now I have people to play with! First, we shake hands, and I use my claws to grasp their fingers. Next, they turn on some music, and we dance together. They make small paper toys for me, and I nibble on a little paper ball. Inside, I find a surprise. There's a treat in the center. I am having so much fun!

Text	Nouns
The Right Pet for Your Home	
My Funny Phone Prank	
Dog Walker Ad	

Name: _____ **Date:** _____

Directions: Closely read these texts. Then, write about the authors' purpose for each of these texts.

Close-Reading Texts

The Right Pet for Your Home	My Funny Phone Prank
Cats can live happily in large or small homes. They need some space to run and play. They also like high places to perch and hide. And they do not need a large outdoor area. Many people keep cats indoors so they can stay safe.	"Just a minute," the father of my family says. "I think I heard the phone ring." He answers it by saying, "Hello?" I make the sound again, and my family looks surprised. Then, they start to laugh. "That wasn't the phone! That was Violet playing a prank!" they say. "What a smart and funny bird!"

Authors' Purpose

Why did the author write the text? What do they want readers to know or learn? How do they want readers to feel?

The Right Pet for Your Home	My Funny Phone Prank
_____ _____ _____ _____	_____ _____ _____ _____

Name: _____ **Date:** _____

Directions: Think about the texts from this unit. Then, respond to the prompt.

You would like to be hired for the dog walker position from the ad. Write what you will say when you call the number on the ad. Think of questions you may have for the owner. What will you say about why you want this job?

_____

_____

_____

_____

_____

_____

_____

_____

_____

_____

Name: _____ **Date:** _____

Directions: You need help with your pet. Design an advertisement. Give details about the following:

- what kind of help is needed
- what kind of pet you have
- what you will need them to do
- when you need them
- how much they will be paid

Name: _____ **Date:** _____

Directions: Read the text, and answer the questions.

 As You Read

Underline information that is new or interesting to you.

Snowy Owl

Snowy owls are beautiful creatures. Their name comes from the color of some of their feathers. They are as white as snow. Male snowy owls grow whiter with age. The females have more dark spots. Snowy owls patiently wait for their prey. They have a keen sense of hearing that helps them catch their next meal.

1. What is the text mostly about?

   (A) snowy owls

   (B) an owl's diet

   (C) snow

   (D) an owl's sense of hearing

2. How are female snowy owls different from males?

   (A) They get whiter as they get older.

   (B) They eat different prey.

   (C) They have more dark spots.

   (D) They have longer feathers.

3. What is the root word in *beautiful*?

   (A) tiful

   (B) beauty

   (C) beau

   (D) ful

4. What does the word *prey* mean?

   (A) nocturnal animals

   (B) smart animals

   (C) meat eaters who eat other animals

   (D) animals hunted by other animals

Name: _____ Date: _____

Directions: Read the text, and answer the questions.

 As You Read

Put a ☆ next to information you already knew.

Moon Phases

The moon is always orbiting around Earth. The moon goes through cycles, which means that our view of the moon changes, even though a whole moon is always in space. Some nights, people on Earth see a full moon. On other nights, they see a half-moon. A quarter-moon looks like a skinny sliver. On some nights, there is no moon to see at all! This is a new moon.

1. Which new title best fits the text?
   - (A) Things That Orbit
   - (B) A Changing, Orbiting Moon
   - (C) Half Moons
   - (D) New Moons Are No Moons

2. Which of the following is true?
   - (A) We only see a full moon in the summer.
   - (B) Our view of the moon changes as it orbits Earth.
   - (C) Different people see different moons.
   - (D) The moon changes shape over time.

3. How many syllables are in the word *orbiting*?
   - (A) one syllable
   - (B) two syllables
   - (C) three syllables
   - (D) four syllables

4. What is it called when no moon can be seen?
   - (A) a new moon
   - (B) a quarter-moon
   - (C) a full moon
   - (D) an empty moon

135044—180 Days of Reading   © Shell Education

Directions: Read the text, and answer the questions.

 As You Read

Draw a ♀ anywhere you have questions or would like more information.

Starry Night

The night sky is beautiful to watch. There are millions of stars to see. Some stars form pictures. People have named those pictures. They are called *constellations*. They make stargazing fun!

1. Which word has the same root word as *named*?

   Ⓐ nominee

   Ⓑ tamed

   Ⓒ rename

   Ⓓ medicine

2. What are constellations?

   Ⓐ the night sky

   Ⓑ the moon in the sky

   Ⓒ stars that form pictures

   Ⓓ stargazing

3. What is the main idea?

   _____

   _____

4. Do you think the night sky is beautiful? Why or why not?

   _____

   _____

   _____

Name: _____   Date: _____

Put an **!** next to information that surprises you.

What Comes Alive at Night

It's the middle of the night. Most people are home in bed. A whole other world of creatures comes alive at night. These creatures are alert. They stay awake at night and sleep during the day. They are called *nocturnal*.

Nocturnal animals have ways to survive at night. They must find food. They also must escape predators. Nocturnal animals may have a strong sense of sight. This helps them see things in the dark. Many nocturnal animals also have strong senses of smell. They can smell food. They can also sense danger.

There are many different nocturnal animals. Cats are one example. Cats can see well in the dark. This helps them spot food. They have excellent hearing, too. They can even hear the high-pitched sounds mice make. Humans cannot hear these pitches. Owls are also nocturnal. They have strong hearing and vision, too. This helps them swoop down on their prey. Owls, like cats, are good hunters.

Directions: Read "What Comes Alive at Night." Then, answer the questions.

1. Which shows a strong connection to the text?
   - (A) My dog likes to go to the dog park.
   - (B) I had an interesting dream last night.
   - (C) I have a cat that likes to explore at night.
   - (D) I get scared by the dark.

2. Which statement is **not** true for nocturnal animals?
   - (A) They have good vision.
   - (B) They sleep at night.
   - (C) They are awake through the night.
   - (D) They have great hearing.

3. Which statement about owls and cats is true?
   - (A) Owls and cats are good hunters.
   - (B) Owls and cats are nocturnal.
   - (C) Owls and cats have strong hearing and vision.
   - (D) all of the above

4. Which summary best describes the text?
   - (A) Nocturnal animals cannot survive at night.
   - (B) Owls are nocturnal. They are good at hunting at night.
   - (C) Nocturnal animals are awake at night. They have strong senses to help them hunt.
   - (D) Owls and cats hunt at night. This means they are nocturnal.

5. Write the main idea and three details from the text.

Main Idea		
Detail	**Detail**	**Detail**

Name: _____ **Date:** _____

Directions: Reread "What Comes Alive at Night." Then, respond to the prompt.

Think about how different creatures are awake at night while you sleep. Do you wonder what they do all night? Choose a nocturnal animal you know of. Write about what you imagine the animal does at night. Your response can be serious or silly. Draw a picture of your animal.

_____

_____

_____

_____

_____

_____

_____

_____

_____

Name: _____ **Date:** _____

Directions: Read the text, and answer the questions.

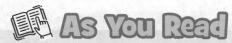
Circle words with long vowel sounds.

How Night Came to Be: Part 1

Many years ago, it was light during the day. It was also light during the night. There was no darkness at all. One day, the Creator needed help with a job. She needed someone who could fly.

"Bat, will you carry this basket to the moon for me?" she asked.

1. Which word from the text has a suffix?
   - (A) basket
   - (B) darkness
   - (C) someone
   - (D) carry

2. What does the Creator need?
   - (A) someone who can sing
   - (B) someone who can see at night
   - (C) someone who can fly
   - (D) someone who is strong

3. Which two words from the text rhyme?
   - (A) *light* and *night*
   - (B) *day* and *darkness*
   - (C) *fly* and *carry*
   - (D) *moon* and *many*

4. Which animal would **not** *work* for this job?
   - (A) bat
   - (B) owl
   - (C) cat
   - (D) firefly

Directions: Read the text, and answer the questions.

Draw an 👁 next to words that help you visualize.

How Night Came to Be: Part 2

Bat did not know what was in the basket. Still, he agreed to the task, so he took it and flew off.

He wanted to fly high up into the bright sky, but the basket was very heavy. He flew low for a while. Before long, he swooped down to rest.

1. Which word has the same vowel sound as in the word *high*?
   - Ⓐ did
   - Ⓑ while
   - Ⓒ still
   - Ⓓ rest

2. Why does Bat fly low for a while?
   - Ⓐ He is hungry.
   - Ⓑ He is tired.
   - Ⓒ He is getting too hot.
   - Ⓓ He is injured.

3. What does Bat do last?
   - Ⓐ He agrees to fly with the basket.
   - Ⓑ He flies low for a while.
   - Ⓒ He swoops down.
   - Ⓓ He flies away.

4. Which is true about this text?
   - Ⓐ Bat gives up.
   - Ⓑ Bat flies high in the sky.
   - Ⓒ Bat flies low in the sky
   - Ⓓ Bat walks with the basket.

Directions: Read the text, and answer the questions.

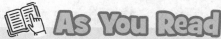 **As You Read**
Think of connections you can make to the text.
Write a ∞ whenever you make connections.

How Night Came to Be: Part 3

Bat landed on the ground. He set the basket down.

This basket is very heavy, he thought to himself. *And the trip to the moon is long.* He decided he needed more energy. He went to find some food.

1. What does Bat do before he sets the basket down?

   Ⓐ thinks to himself

   Ⓑ goes to find some food

   Ⓒ lands on the ground

   Ⓓ takes a trip to the moon

2. Why does Bat go look for food?

   Ⓐ He needs more energy.

   Ⓑ He wants food for the flight.

   Ⓒ He is thirsty.

   Ⓓ He is getting it for the Creator.

3. What is one way you get more energy when you are tired?

   _____

   _____

4. How is Bat feeling about the trip to the moon so far?

   _____

   _____

As You Read
Draw a ♡ next to your favorite part(s) of the story.

How Night Came to Be: Part 4

While Bat was gone, Owl and Fox spotted the basket. They wondered what was inside. Fox sniffed it and Owl tried to push it over.

"Should we open it?" Fox asked.

"It is not ours," Owl answered.

But they were so curious, and they could not resist the mystery. They had to open the basket! Together, they lifted the top. Darkness flew out! Owl and Fox watched as it spread all over the sky.

Just then, Bat was on his way back. He gasped upon seeing the open basket.

"What have you done?" he cried, swooping in.

Startled, Owl and Fox ran away. Bat looked around and saw only darkness. He flew and flew trying to gather it up. *It will take all night to put it back in the basket!* he thought. *And there is so much of it! It will never fit back in!*

From that time on, Bat had a new job to do. He rested during the day so he could work at night. All night, he gathered the darkness and put it in the basket. By morning, it was light again. But the darkness was tricky. Each time Bat pushed the last bit into the basket, the other end of the basket cracked open. Darkness slowly escaped through the crack. By nighttime, it was dark again.

Name: _____ **Date:** _____

Directions: Read "How Night Came to Be: Part 4." Then, answer the questions.

1. What flies out of the basket?

    (A) leftover food

    (B) darkness

    (C) light

    (D) nothing

2. Who sniffs the basket?

    (A) Fox

    (B) Bat

    (C) Owl

    (D) nobody

3. What is the meaning of the word *startled*?

    (A) smiled

    (B) quiet

    (C) surprised

    (D) hungry

4. What is Bat's new job?

    (A) gathering darkness

    (B) gathering light

    (C) finding food for Fox and Owl

    (D) flying to the moon each night

5. Describe the problem and solution in the story.

Problem	Solution

Name: _____ **Date:** _____

Directions: Reread "How Night Came to Be: Part 4." Then, respond to the prompt.

> What if Fox and Owl had never opened the basket? Rewrite this part of the story. Add your own ending that tells how darkness was created.

_____

_____

_____

_____

_____

_____

_____

_____

_____

_____

_____

Am I Nocturnal?

Many people think so.
And they get scared when
they see me in the day.
But I'm actually diurnal.
That means I'm active in
the day and at night.

So don't worry if you see
me out and about. But
please, keep your distance!

Name: _____ **Date:** _____

Directions: Read the animal poster on page 77. Then, answer the questions.

1. Which sentence has the correct punctuation?

   Ⓐ Am I nocturnal.

   Ⓑ Am I nocturnal?

   Ⓒ Am I nocturnal!

   Ⓓ "Am I nocturnal"

2. What animal is the poster referring to?

   Ⓐ rat

   Ⓑ skunk

   Ⓒ raccoon

   Ⓓ squirrel

3. Which sentence is a warning to readers?

   Ⓐ "But I'm actually diurnal."

   Ⓑ "That means I'm active in the day and at night."

   Ⓒ "So don't worry if you see me out and about."

   Ⓓ "But please, keep your distance!"

4. What is the root word in *scared*?

   Ⓐ scar

   Ⓑ scare

   Ⓒ red

   Ⓓ are

5. What does *diurnal* mean?

   _____

   _____

   _____

135044—180 Days of Reading   © Shell Education

Name: _____ **Date:** _____

Directions: Closely read these texts. Then, study the poster on page 77. Look for words with two syllables in each text. Write the words in the chart.

Close-Reading Texts

What Comes Alive at Night	How Night Came to Be: Part 4
It's the middle of the night. Most people are home in bed. A whole other world of creatures comes alive at night. These creatures are alert. They stay awake at night and sleep during the day. They are called *nocturnal*.	While Bat was gone, Owl and Fox spotted the basket. They wondered what was inside. Fox sniffed it and Owl tried to push it over. "Should we open it?" Fox asked. "It is not ours," Owl answered. But they were so curious, and they could not resist the mystery. They had to open the basket!

Text	Two-Syllable Words
What Comes Alive at Night	
How Night Came to Be: Part 4	
Animal Poster	

Name: _____ Date: _____

Directions: Closely read these texts. Then, write about the authors' purpose for each of these texts.

Close-Reading Texts

What Comes Alive at Night	How Night Came to Be: Part 4
There are many different nocturnal animals. Cats are one example. Cats can see well in the darkness. This helps them spot food. They have excellent hearing, too. They can even hear the high-pitched sounds mice make. Humans cannot hear these pitches.	All night, he gathered the darkness and put it in the basket. By morning, it was light again. But the darkness was tricky. Each time Bat pushed the last bit into the basket, the other end of the basket cracked open. Darkness slowly escaped through the crack. By nighttime, it was dark again.

Authors' Purpose

Why did the author write the text? What do they want readers to know or learn? How do they want readers to feel?

What Comes Alive at Night	How Night Came to Be: Part 4
_____	_____
_____	_____
_____	_____
_____	_____
_____	_____

Name: _____ **Date:** _____

Directions: Think about the texts from this unit. Then, respond to the prompt.

Think of a time when you touched or played with something you were not supposed to. What happened? How did the situation end? How was it similar to what happened to Bat?

_____

_____

_____

_____

_____

_____

_____

_____

_____

_____

Name: _____ **Date:** _____

Directions: Create your own nocturnal animal. Give it a name and list its special characteristics. Then, make a poster telling all about your animal.

Name: _____

Characteristics: _____

_____

Name: _____   Date: _____

Directions: Read the text, then answer the questions.

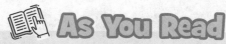

Underline information that is new or interesting to you.

Which Way?

Compasses show direction. They show where north, south, east, and west are. Compasses have been used for a long time. Ships used to rely on compasses. Compasses told them which way to travel. People still use compasses today. They are smaller. They are easier to use. Most cell phones even have a compass app.

1. What is the main idea?

   Ⓐ travel

   Ⓑ direction

   Ⓒ compasses

   Ⓓ ships

2. Which idea is **not** suggested in this text?

   Ⓐ A compass shows direction.

   Ⓑ A compass is a globe.

   Ⓒ A compass tells people which way to travel.

   Ⓓ Compasses have been used for a long time.

3. Which word has the same root word as *smaller*?

   Ⓐ smallest

   Ⓑ biggest

   Ⓒ taller

   Ⓓ smell

4. What is one way compasses are different today than long ago?

   Ⓐ They are larger.

   Ⓑ They are easier to use.

   Ⓒ They are harder to use.

   Ⓓ They are only on cell phones.

Directions: Read the text, then answer the questions.

Write a **?** where you would like more information.

Size It Up

A lake on a map should not look larger than an ocean! This is why drawing to scale is important. It means that objects are sized as they look next to other objects. Artists think about scale. So do architects. They draw designs to scale. Mapmakers work with scale, too.

These animals are not drawn to scale.

These animals are drawn to scale.

1. Which new title best captures the main idea?

- (A) Lakes and Oceans
- (B) Drawing to Scale
- (C) A Mapmaker's Work
- (D) An Artist's Skill

2. What is the text mostly about?

- (A) maps
- (B) scale
- (C) architects
- (D) artists

3. Which word has the same vowel sound as *lake*?

- (A) look
- (B) large
- (C) make
- (D) draw

4. Which definition of *scale* is used in this text?

- (A) fish skin
- (B) weighing machine
- (C) climb
- (D) correct size

Name: _____ **Date:** _____

Directions: Read the text, then answer the questions.

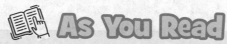 **As You Read**

Put a ☆ next to information you already knew.

Ever-Changing World

A globe is a model of Earth. It is in the shape of a sphere. Globes must be updated over time. They must show what the world looks like today. Countries' borders shift, and names can change. Sometimes, a lake or a river even disappears. The world never stays the same.

1. Which word has the same vowel sound as the word *change*.
   - (A) globe
   - (B) lake
   - (C) must
   - (D) world

2. Which of these words have similar meanings?
   - (A) *update* and *change*
   - (B) *shift* and *disappear*
   - (C) *shape* and *world*
   - (D) *model* and *sphere*

3. What is the main idea?

   _____

   _____

4. Why do you think the image of the globe has different colors?

   _____

   _____

   _____

   _____

Name: _____   Date: _____

 **As You Read**

Draw a ☆ next to important or interesting facts about maps.

Parts of a Map

Maps show people information. Maps are visual pictures that represent places. There are many different types of maps. Maps can show locations. They may tell people where to find city roads. They can show where a river flows. Maps can even show changes in the weather. Maps tell us a lot about the world around us.

Maps show objects as symbols. For example, a road might be shown as a black line on a map. A park might be shown as a tree. A school might be shown as a bell. These symbols are found in a key. The key tells what each symbol means. A key is also called a *legend*.

Maps also have compass roses. The compass rose shows direction. It shows north and south. It shows east and west, too. People who use maps rely on the compass rose to show them direction. It reminds them where places are compared to other places.

Maps have to be fairly small to be usable. A map of a country cannot be as big as a real country! This is where drawing to scale comes in. A map drawn to scale is smaller than what it shows. It accurately shows the size of roads or locations.

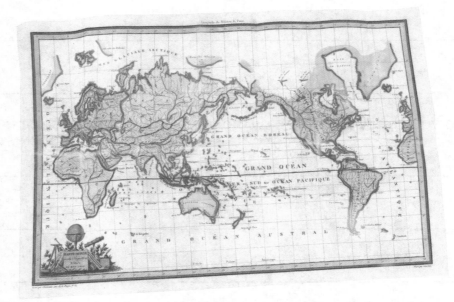

Directions: Read "Parts of a Map." Then, answer the questions.

1. What is the meaning of *key* in this text?

  (A) a legend

  (B) a metal object

  (C) a compass

  (D) a scale

2. What is **not** usually shown on a map?

  (A) rivers

  (B) countries

  (C) city roads

  (D) people

3. Why are maps drawn to scale?

  (A) to make them look pretty

  (B) to make them as small as possible

  (C) because the true size of objects would be too big

  (D) because it's more fun

4. Which two words from the text rhyme?

  (A) *north* and *south*

  (B) *bell* and *tell*

  (C) *place* and *park*

  (D) *east* and *west*

5. Write the main idea of the text. Write three details.

Main Idea

Detail	Detail	Detail

Name: _____ **Date:** _____

Directions: Reread "Parts of a Map." Then, respond to one of the prompts.

1. Write about a time when you got to use a map. Was it helpful?
2. Write about a time you wish you had a map. How would it have helped?

_____

_____

_____

_____

_____

_____

_____

_____

_____

_____

_____

Name: _____ Date: _____

Directions: Read the text, then answer the questions.

 **As You Read**

Think of connections you can make to the text.
Write a ∞ whenever you make connections.

Playing Pirate

My friend Derek is over at my house. Our parents think we are playing on the swing set and playing tag in the backyard. But we're not. We're real-life pirates!

We sail on boats, and we fight with swords! We make up pirate songs and sing them out loud!

1. What do the kids' parents think they are doing outside?
   - (A) playing on the swing set
   - (B) playing pirates
   - (C) riding bikes
   - (D) playing hide and seek

2. What activity do the pirates **not** play?
   - (A) sail on boats
   - (B) fight with swords
   - (C) make eye patches
   - (D) sing pirate songs

3. Which word has the same vowel sound as *out*?
   - (A) sing
   - (B) over
   - (C) loud
   - (D) make

4. Which word does not have a suffix?
   - (A) playing
   - (B) pirate
   - (C) loudly
   - (D) fighter

Name: _____   Date: _____

Directions: Read the text, then answer the questions.

 **As You Read**
Circle words with long vowel sounds.

Another Word for Yes

We say "Arrr!" Do you want to know why? That's our special way of saying "Yes!" when we're excited.

Derek and I are busy playing in the backyard when my mom calls out to us from the back door.

"Angelo and Derek! Would you like a cupcake?" she asks. We answer her using pirate language.

"Arrr!" we say, laughing.

1. According to the kids, what does *Arrr* mean in pirate language?
Ⓐ Come here.
Ⓑ No.
Ⓒ Yes.
Ⓓ I don't know.

2. What word means the same as *excited*?
Ⓐ thrilled
Ⓑ upset
Ⓒ confused
Ⓓ sad

3. What is another good title for this text?
Ⓐ Backyard Kids
Ⓑ Pirate Language
Ⓒ A Special Way
Ⓓ Mom's Smile

4. Which word from the text is a compound word?
Ⓐ special
Ⓑ excited
Ⓒ cupcake
Ⓓ pirate

Name: _____ Date: _____

Directions: Read the text, and answer the questions.

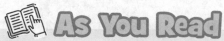

Draw a rectangle around new or interesting vocabulary words.

Burying Our Loot

I have a bag full of beautiful, shiny pennies. This is our pirate's loot! We will bury it in a secret place. I will use my garden tools to dig a hole and cover it up. No one will ever find our treasure.

But wait—will we forget where it is buried? I think we'd better make a map!

1. What is the singular form of *pennies*?
   - (A) penne
   - (B) penny
   - (C) pennie
   - (D) penni

2. Which word does **not** have two syllables?
   - (A) garden
   - (B) pirate
   - (C) place
   - (D) treasure

3. What does the narrator use to bury the loot?

_____

_____

4. What does the narrator do so they don't forget where the loot is buried?

_____

_____

Name: _____   Date: _____

As You Read

Write an **S** whenever you identify a part of the setting.

A Real Treasure Map

Look what we've found. It's another pirate's treasure map! Now we can search for the treasure and steal it because that's what pirates do!

"What if we're caught?" Derek asks.

"We'll have a duel and fight them off with our swords," I answer, "but let's hurry just in case!"

The map shows landmarks in my backyard. My house and swing set are both on it, and arrows point us where we need to go.

"This way!" I say, and Derek and I run across the lawn.

We follow the map to the front yard and over to the big tree. We go past the porch swing, around the mailbox, and everywhere it tells us to go. At the end, it takes us to a large pot outside the back door. The map has a drawing of the pot crossed out with a big red X on it. The pot is filled with fresh dirt.

"This is it!" Derek says. "Let's dig!"

I use my garden tools again and dig in the dirt in the pot. My shovel hits something, so I reach in and pull it out. It's a box. No, it's a treasure chest! I open it up, and I find four cupcakes inside of it!

"Two for you and two for me," I say, passing them to Derek. The chocolate frosting and rainbow sprinkles on top are making my mouth water. We are real pirates who found real treasure. And I think my mom might be a pirate, too!

Directions: Read "A Real Treasure Map." Then, answer the questions.

1. What is the pot filled with?

Ⓐ flowers

Ⓑ dirt

Ⓒ a tree

Ⓓ toys

2. What is inside the "treasure chest"?

Ⓐ cookies

Ⓑ cupcakes

Ⓒ dirt

Ⓓ nothing

3. What symbol on the map has an *X* marked on it?

Ⓐ the back door

Ⓑ the tree

Ⓒ the pot

Ⓓ the shovel

4. Which word from the text is **not** a compound word?

Ⓐ backyard

Ⓑ landmark

Ⓒ garden

Ⓓ outside

5. Write about four major events. Put them in the order they occur in the story.

Event 1	
Event 2	
Event 3	
Event 4	

Directions: Reread "A Real Treasure Map." Then, respond to the prompt.

What connections did you make with the text? Playing with friends? Being creative? Think of a specific connection (or two). Explain them in detail.

_____

_____

_____

_____

_____

_____

_____

_____

_____

_____

How to Be a Kind Pirate

1. Say "Arrr!" a lot.
2. Threaten to make people walk the plank (but don't really do it).
3. If you steal treasure, be sure to give it back.
4. Bury treasure and make a map for other pirates to follow.

Name: _____ **Date:** _____

Directions: Read "How to Be a Kind Pirate." Then, answer the questions.

1. What is the meaning of the word *steal*?

   Ⓐ borrow

   Ⓑ take

   Ⓒ give

   Ⓓ receive

2. Which step involves making something?

   Ⓐ 1

   Ⓑ 2

   Ⓒ 3

   Ⓓ 4

3. What should a kind pirate do after stealing treasure?

   Ⓐ Walk the plank.

   Ⓑ Say "Arrr" a lot.

   Ⓒ Give it back.

   Ⓓ Make a map.

4. Which word has more than one syllable?

   Ⓐ make

   Ⓑ bury

   Ⓒ walk

   Ⓓ plank

5. What else would you add to this list? Write as many ideas as you can.

   _____

   _____

   _____

   _____

   _____

   _____

   _____

Directions: Closely read these texts. Then, study the list on page 95. Look for nouns in each text. Write the words in the chart.

Close-Reading Texts

Parts of a Map	A Real Treasure Map
Maps show people information. Maps are visual pictures that represent places. There are many different types of maps. Maps can show locations. They may tell people where to find city roads. They can show where a river flows. Maps can even show changes in the weather. Maps tell us a lot about the world around us.	Look what we've found. It's another pirate's treasure map! Now we can search for the treasure and steal it because that's what pirates do! "What if we're caught?" Derek asks. "We'll have a duel and fight them off with our swords," I answer, "but let's hurry just in case!" The map shows landmarks in my backyard. My house and swing set are both on it, and arrows point us where we need to go.

Text	Nouns
Parts of a Map	
A Real Treasure Map	
Kind Pirate List	

Name: _____ **Date:** _____

Directions: Closely read these texts. Then, write about the authors' purpose for each of these texts.

Close-Reading Texts

Parts of a Map	A Real Treasure Map
The compass rose shows direction. It shows north and south. It shows east and west, too. People who use maps rely on the compass rose to show them direction. It reminds them where places are compared to other places. Maps have to be fairly small to be usable. A map of a country cannot be as big as a real country! This is where drawing to scale comes in.	My shovel hits something, so I reach in and pull it out. It's a box. No, it's a treasure chest! I open it up, and I find four cupcakes inside of it! "Two for you and two for me," I say, passing them to Derek. The chocolate frosting and rainbow sprinkles on top are making my mouth water. We are real pirates who found real treasure. And I think my mom might be a pirate, too!

Authors' Purpose
Why did the author write the text? What do they want readers to know or learn? How do they want readers to feel?

Parts of a Map	A Real Treasure Map

Directions: Think about the texts from this unit. Then, respond to the prompt.

Imagine you are a pirate. Write a letter to a fellow pirate friend. Tell the pirate what you've been up to. Ask about the pirate's latest adventures. Ask for advice on how to become a better pirate. Get creative!

_____

_____,

_____

_____

_____

_____

_____

_____

_____,

_____

Name: _____ **Date:** _____

Directions: Create a map of your bedroom. Be sure to include a key with symbols. Draw it to scale as best you can. Then, write steps that tell how to make a map.

_____

_____

_____

_____

Directions: Read the text, and answer the questions.

 **As You Read**

Draw a ❓ anywhere you have questions or would like more information.

Go Kart Go

Many kids want to be race car drivers. They like the idea of going fast. They think cars are exciting and fun. Some kids get started early. They build small go-karts. This can be a fun thing to do with an adult or older sibling. It is essential to follow a good plan!

1. What is the text mostly about?

　Ⓐ following a plan

　Ⓑ working together with a parent

　Ⓒ cars and go-karts

　Ⓓ hobbies

2. How do some kids get an early start in race car driving?

　Ⓐ They spend time outside.

　Ⓑ They run fast.

　Ⓒ They find a hobby.

　Ⓓ They build go-karts.

3. What is the root word in *exciting*?

　Ⓐ excite

　Ⓑ exci

　Ⓒ ting

　Ⓓ citi

4. What word can be used instead of *essential* in the last sentence?

　Ⓐ decision

　Ⓑ important

　Ⓒ awful

　Ⓓ confusing

Name: _____ Date: _____

Directions: Read the text, then answer the questions.

Put a ☆ next to information you already knew.

Track and Field

Track and field is a sport. It includes running, jumping, and throwing. Athletes compete in a stadium. There is a large oval track. Runners race around the track. Some races are long. The longest race is over six miles (10 kilometers). Other races are very short. They are sprints. They may take less than 20 seconds!

1. Which title best fits the text?
- (A) Jumping for Sport
- (B) Around the Track
- (C) Facts About Track and Field
- (D) Running Six Miles

2. Which statement is true about track and field?
- (A) All runners do six-mile races.
- (B) It includes running, jumping, and throwing.
- (C) Long races are called sprints.
- (D) Track and field is only indoors.

3. How many syllables are in the word *compete*?
- (A) one syllable
- (B) two syllables
- (C) three syllables
- (D) four syllables

4. Which would probably **not** take place in a stadium?
- (A) a track and field meet
- (B) a professional baseball game
- (C) a classroom play
- (D) a rock concert

Directions: Read the text, and answer the questions.

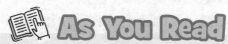 **As You Read**

Underline information that is new or interesting to you.

Clean Cars

Most cars run on gas. Gas engines create exhaust. This can make the air dirty. This is called *pollution*. Some cars are cleaner. Hybrids are one example. They run on gas, but they also use battery power. They use less gas than regular cars. This makes them better for the environment.

1. Based on the text, why are hybrids better for the environment?

   Ⓐ They run on gas.

   Ⓑ They use less gas and create less pollution.

   Ⓒ They have a gas engine.

   Ⓓ They do not make any pollution.

2. Which word has the same root word as *pollution*?

   Ⓐ polluted

   Ⓑ poll

   Ⓒ lotion

   Ⓓ potion

3. What do most cars run on?

   _____

4. What is exhaust? Use clues in the text to help you.

   _____

   _____

As You Read

Underline information that is new or intersting to you.

The Racetrack

Henry Ford is a famous man. He made cars. He formed a company. It was the Ford Motor Company. He started it in 1903. It is still making cars today! Cars grew more popular after Ford created his company. More people could afford to buy cars. Cars changed the way that people lived. Over time, people grew to love their cars. Today, many people drive every day.

Auto racing began around the 1900s. A new sport was born. People enjoyed watching cars race. The National Association for Stock Car Racing (NASCAR) was formed in 1948. The sport has changed over time. Cars used to race on dirt tracks. Now, they mostly race on pavement. The shapes of the tracks have changed, too. Now, they are oval. They also have steep sides. This track design helps cars go faster. The cars are safer now, too.

Henry Ford might be surprised if he were alive today. His dream has taken off!

Directions: Read "The Racetrack." Then, answer the questions.

1. Which experience would help you better understand the text?

   (A) I paint toy cars with my dad every weekend.

   (B) I like to walk with my neighbor.

   (C) I have watched NASCAR races on TV.

   (D) When I am old enough, I will buy a motorcycle.

2. In what year was NASCAR formed?

   (A) 1900

   (B) 1903

   (C) 1928

   (D) 1948

3. What shape is a racetrack today?

   (A) a circle

   (B) an oval

   (C) a square

   (D) a rectangle

4. Which statement gives the best summary of the text?

   (A) The Ford Motor Company is still around today.

   (B) NASCAR was formed in 1948.

   (C) Henry Ford's invention has created a popular and thrilling sport.

   (D) Henry Ford made a car that was designed for everyone.

5. Write four facts about Henry Ford.

Henry Ford

Name: _____ **Date:** _____

Directions: Reread "The Racetrack." Then, respond to the prompt.

Imagine you are driving a race car. Describe what it is like. Tell what you see, feel, and think. Draw a picture to go with your writing.

_____

_____

_____

_____

_____

_____

_____

Directions: Read the text, then answer the questions.

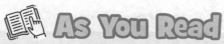 **As You Read**

Draw a rectangle around new or interesting words.

A Special Scout Meeting

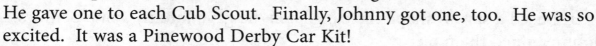

Johnny always liked going to Cub Scout meetings. But this meeting was extra special. The Scoutmaster had a big box with him. He reached into it.

"Everyone will get one," he announced. "Please be patient."

What was in the box? Johnny could hardly wait to find out. The Scoutmaster made his way around the room. He pulled smaller boxes out of the large box. He gave one to each Cub Scout. Finally, Johnny got one, too. He was so excited. It was a Pinewood Derby Car Kit!

1. Why is this meeting extra special?
   - (A) It is Johnny's birthday.
   - (B) It is camping day.
   - (C) The scoutmaster has a surprise.
   - (D) It is race day!

2. Which word does **not** have a suffix?
   - (A) finally
   - (B) special
   - (C) hardly
   - (D) smaller

3. How does Johnny feel when he gets his box?
   - (A) sad
   - (B) confused
   - (C) happy
   - (D) upset

4. Which word has the opposite meaning of *patient*?
   - (A) kind
   - (B) impatient
   - (C) helpful
   - (D) excited

Name: _____ Date: _____

Directions: Read the text, then answer the questions.

Draw an 👁 next to words that help you visualize the text.

Striving for Speed

Johnny and his dad took the kit home. They opened the box and took out the pieces. There was a block of wood for the car's body, wheels, axles, and stickers to decorate with.

"How can we make it go really fast?" Johnny asked. He wanted to win the upcoming race!

"Let's make the block into a wedge," his dad suggested, "and we can add weight to it, too."

He used a saw to shape the car. Then, he gave Johnny some pennies. Johnny glued them on.

1. What do Johnny and his dad do after they open the box?
   - (A) They get some pennies.
   - (B) Johnny glues pennies on the car.
   - (C) They take the pieces out of the box.
   - (D) They take the kit home.

2. What is **not** included in the box?
   - (A) wheels
   - (B) pennies
   - (C) axles
   - (D) stickers

3. What do they use to shape the block of wood into a car?
   - (A) sandpaper
   - (B) a knife
   - (C) glue
   - (D) a saw

4. What shape do they decide to make the car?
   - (A) a wedge
   - (B) a circle
   - (C) a square
   - (D) a rectangle

Name: _____ **Date:** _____

Directions: Read the text, then answer the questions.

 **As You Read**
Think of connections you can make to the text.
Write a ∞ whenever you make connections.

A Fierce Design

The pieces of the car were all put together. Now Johnny can decorate! He chose a theme. He wanted the car to look like his favorite animal. So, Johnny painted the wood orange. He added black stripes. The front needed a face. He used black paint for eyes and white paint for teeth. In the end, his car looked like a tiger!

1. Why does Johnny choose orange and black for his car?

- (A) He loves Halloween.
- (B) Orange is his favorite color.
- (C) He wants it to look like a tiger.
- (D) Black is his favorite color.

2. Which word has more than two syllables?

- (A) tiger
- (B) animal
- (C) wanted
- (D) theme

3. What is Johnny's favorite animal?

_____

4. How would you decorate your own toy car?

_____

_____

_____

Draw an 👁 whenever there is a good visual.

Race Day!

On Saturday, Johnny and his father brought his car to the school. They went into the gym where the Cub Scouts were gathered with all their cars. They were ready to race! Johnny liked the cars he saw. One was painted with flames on the sides. Another looked like a candy bar. His friend, Tyo, had a cool car. It looked like an ice cream cone.

"Your car is awesome," he told Tyo.

The Scoutmaster announced it was time to race. Johnny put his car on the track. Other cars lined up beside it. The Scoutmaster pulled a lever, and the cars shot down the track. The race was over in a flash. Johnny's car was the fastest! That meant he got to race again. Tyo was in the race again, too. This time, Tyo's car won!

At the end of the day, Tyo's car was the fastest of all, so he won a trophy. Johnny was proud of his friend and congratulated him.

"Great job!" he said. Then the Scoutmaster announced more awards.

"Best Animal Car goes to Johnny!" he said. Johnny was a winner, too!

Best Animal Car

135044—180 Days of Reading

Name: _____ **Date:** _____

Directions: Read "Race Day!" Then, answer the questions.

1. What does Tyo's car look like?

(A) a tiger

(B) an ice cream cone

(C) flames

(D) a candy bar

2. What does this sentence mean?
The race was over in a flash.

(A) It was very bright outside.

(B) The race was hot.

(C) It was a quick race.

(D) The race was very slow.

3. Which detail shows good sportsmanship?

(A) Johnny sees other cars.

(B) The Scoutmaster announces it is time to race.

(C) Johnny puts his car on the track.

(D) Johnny congratulates his friend.

4. Which word has the same vowel as the word *best*?

(A) first

(B) cool

(C) end

(D) paint

5. Describe the beginning, middle, and end of the story.

Beginning	Middle	End

Directions: Reread "Race Day!" Then, respond to the prompt.

Do you like how the story ended? If so, explain why you liked it. If not, write a different ending to the story. Then, write why you changed it.

_____

_____

_____

_____

_____

_____

_____

_____

_____

_____

Name: _____ **Date:** _____

Rules for Building Your Pinewood Derby Car

1. Width must not exceed $2\frac{3}{4}$ inches (7 centimeters).

2. Length must not exceed 7 inches (18 centimeters).

3. Weight must not exceed 5 ounces (0.1 kilograms).

Name: _____ **Date:** _____

Directions: Read "Rules for Building Your Pinewood Derby Car." Then, answer the questions.

1. Which word is a compound word?
   - (A) derby
   - (B) building
   - (C) pinewood
   - (D) exceed

2. Which rule discusses how heavy the car can be?
   - (A) rule 1
   - (B) rule 2
   - (C) rule 3
   - (D) rule 4

3. Which word has the opposite meaning of *build*?
   - (A) make
   - (B) destroy
   - (C) collect
   - (D) connect

4. What is the purpose of this text?
   - (A) to entertain readers
   - (B) to explain how to do something
   - (C) to advertise something
   - (D) to share an opinion

5. What are one or two things you would add to the brochure? Explain your thinking.

_____

_____

_____

_____

_____

_____

Name: _____ **Date:** _____

Directions: Closely read these texts. Then, study the rules on page 113. Look for words with long *a* vowel sounds in each text. Write the words in the chart.

Close-Reading Texts

The Racetrack	Race Day
Henry Ford is a famous man. He made cars. He formed a company. It was the Ford Motor Company. He started it in 1903. It is still making cars today! Cars grew more popular after Ford created his company. More people could afford to buy cars.	On Saturday, Johnny and his father brought his car to the school. They went into the gym where the Cub Scouts were gathered with all their cars. They were ready to race! Johnny liked the cars he saw.

Text	Words with long /a/ vowel sounds
The Racetrack	
The Race	
Brochure	

Name: _____ Date: _____

Directions: Closely read these texts. Then, draw the setting from each paragraph. Write one way they are similar. Write one way they are different.

Close-Reading Texts

The Racetrack	Race Day
The sport has changed over time. Cars used to race on dirt tracks. Now, they mostly race on pavement. The shapes of the tracks have changed, too. Now, they are oval. They also have steep sides. This track design helps cars go faster. The cars are safer now, too. Henry Ford might be surprised if he were alive today. His dream has taken off!	At the end of the day, Tyo's car was the fastest of all, so he won a trophy. Johnny was proud of his friend and congratulated him. "Great job!" he said. Then the Scoutmaster announced more awards. "Best Animal Car goes to Johnny!" he said. Johnny was a winner, too!

1. _____

_____

_____

2. _____

_____

_____

Name: _____ **Date:** _____

Directions: Think about the texts from this unit. Then, respond to the prompt.

> Write a letter to Mr. Henry Ford. Thank him for his invention of the car. Give details about how this invention has affected your life. Ask him some questions.

_____

_____,

_____

_____

_____

_____

_____

_____

_____,

_____

Unit 6 WEEK 3 DAY 4

© Shell Education

135044—180 Days of Reading

Name: _____ **Date:** _____

Directions: Think of something you know how to do. Write directions for how to do what you chose. Write it in a list of steps. Draw a picture to help explain what to do.

_____

_____

_____

_____

_____

_____

Name: _____ **Date:** _____

Directions: Read the text, then answer the questions.

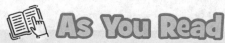 As You Read

Put a **?** anywhere you have a question.

What Can Robots Do?

Robots are all around us. Some help at home. They do chores for people. They vacuum and iron. They wash windows.

Other robots work in different places. They work in restaurants. They cook food. Some of them serve it to customers. They work in factories. They build car parts. Or they help with packaging. They even work in hospitals. They can perform surgery.

Robots are very helpful. They can do almost anything!

1. What is another word for *help*?
   - (A) ignore
   - (B) assist
   - (C) work
   - (D) play

2. According to this text, robots can _____.
   - (A) vacuum
   - (B) cook food
   - (C) perform surgery
   - (D) all of the above

3. What is the singular form of the word *factories*?
   - (A) factor
   - (B) factory
   - (C) fact
   - (D) actor

4. Which word is **not** a verb?
   - (A) help
   - (B) wash
   - (C) robot
   - (D) work

Name: _____ Date: _____

Directions: Read the text, then answer the questions.

 As You Read

Underline information that is new or interesting to you.

Robot Pets

Not all robots work. Some play instead! Pet robots look like cats, dogs, and other animals. Have you ever wanted a pet lion? A real one is impossible. But you could have a robotic lion. Robotic pets move and make sounds. They behave like live animals. Some are covered in fake fur. You can pet them. They respond to voice commands, too.

1. Which word has two syllables?
   - (A) robot
   - (B) pet
   - (C) animal
   - (D) fake

2. Which animal is **not** usually a pet?
   - (A) dog
   - (B) lion
   - (C) cat
   - (D) hamster

3. Which word has a long *i* sound?
   - (A) instead
   - (B) animal
   - (C) voice
   - (D) like

4. Which is **not** a characteristic of an animal robot?
   - (A) They have fake fur.
   - (B) They can move.
   - (C) They eat food.
   - (D) They can make sounds.

Name: _____   Date: _____

Directions: Read the text, then answer the questions.

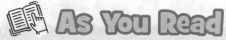 **As You Read**

Underline information that is new to you.

Insect Robots

Robots can look like bugs. The first robot bug looked like a dragonfly. It was a top-secret project that was built long ago. It was made to be a government spy that could listen to people.

There are toy robot bugs, too. They creep and crawl. They move by vibrating. Some of them can fly.

1. Which word rhymes with *spy*?

   Ⓐ like   Ⓒ some

   Ⓑ fly   Ⓓ secret

2. The text says robot bugs can _____.

   Ⓐ talk   Ⓒ crawl

   Ⓑ jump   Ⓓ sing

3. What did the first robot bug look like?

   _____

   _____

4. How do the robot bugs move?

   _____

   _____

Name: _____   Date: _____

 **As You Read**

Put a ☆ next to information you already knew.

The Mars Rovers

There are even robots in space! Five rovers are on Mars. Rovers are robotic vehicles. They move around and take pictures. They carry tools to study rocks, wind, and weather. They help people learn about Mars.

The first rover landed in 1997. It found information about the environment. It found that Mars was not always cold and dry. It was once warm and wet. Two more rovers arrived six years later. They learned about the past. Mars used to have lakes. It had rivers.

Nine more years went by. Then, a fourth rover came. People had been wondering if life could survive on Mars. The rover searched for signs. It found that conditions there are dangerous. It would make life hard. A fifth rover landed in 2021. It is looking for clues. People want to find out if there was life on Mars long ago. It is also helping to plan ahead for future visits.

It might be possible to safely spend time on Mars in the future. Would you like to visit Mars one day?

Directions: Read "The Mars Rovers." Then, answer the questions.

1. Rovers on Mars study _____.

   Ⓐ rocks

   Ⓑ wind

   Ⓒ weather

   Ⓓ all of the above

2. Which is **not** a description of Mars?

   Ⓐ cold

   Ⓑ dry

   Ⓒ snowy

   Ⓓ warm

3. What are rovers?

   Ⓐ toy cars

   Ⓑ robotic vehicles

   Ⓒ large bikes

   Ⓓ machines

4. Which word has a suffix?

   Ⓐ safely

   Ⓑ study

   Ⓒ weather

   Ⓓ carry

5. Write the four major events about the Mars rovers landing on Mars. Write them in the order they occurred.

Event 1	
Event 2	
Event 3	
Event 4	

Name: _____ **Date:** _____

Directions: Reread "The Mars Rovers." Then, respond to the prompt.

Think about what it would be like to go to the planet Mars. Write about what you might see, study, or do while there. Tell how you might use the Mars rover. Draw a picture to go with your writing.

_____

_____

_____

_____

_____

_____

_____

Name: _____ Date: _____

Directions: Read the text, then answer the questions.

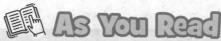 **As You Read**

Think of connections you can make to the text.
Write a ∞ whenever you make connections.

The Assistant

"I want to invent a robot to have as an assistant," Nate told his mom.

"What would your robot do?" his mom asked.

"It would clean my room," he said. "Actually, it would do all my chores."

"That sounds nice! Let me know when you invent him because I want him to do my housework, too," his mom said.

1. Who is having a conversation?
- (A) Nate and his friend
- (B) a mother and a robot
- (C) Nate and his mother
- (D) a boy and a robot

2. What is the text mostly about?
- (A) inventing a robot assistant
- (B) doing chores
- (C) plans to clean a room
- (D) plans for doing homework

3. Which word is a compound word?
- (A) wondered
- (B) assistant
- (C) housework
- (D) actually

4. Which words are synonyms?
- (A) *clean* and *claimed*
- (B) *invent* and *assistant*
- (C) *chores* and *invent*
- (D) *housework* and *chores*

Directions: Read the text, then answer the questions.

Put an **!** next to information that surprises you.

Yes or No?

Nina wondered if her life was easier than her parents' lives were at her age. She knew her parents' stories. She knew they did not have what she has. They had fewer channels to watch on TV. There were no video games or computers. *What would it have been like?* Nina thought. *Is life easier with technology?*

1. What does Nina wonder about?
   - (A) how much TV to watch
   - (B) whether life is easier with technology
   - (C) whether to buy a new computer
   - (D) when to watch TV

2. What is this text mostly about?
   - (A) a girl who complains about her hard life
   - (B) a girl who thinks about how technology has changed life
   - (C) a girl who knows her parents' stories
   - (D) a girl who does not like computers

3. How many syllables are in the word *technology*?
   - (A) five syllables
   - (B) two syllables
   - (C) three syllables
   - (D) four syllables

4. What would **not** be considered technology?
   - (A) video games
   - (B) computers
   - (C) cable television
   - (D) printed books

Name: _____ **Date:** _____

Directions: Read the text, then answer the questions.

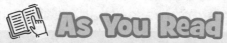 As You Read

Draw an 👁 next to words that help you visualize the text.

Forks Up!

The android was confused by what he saw as he looked through the telescope. What object was he looking at? It had pointy ends and a handle. It looked like humans were poking their food. They used the object to stick the food into their mouths. What in the world was this crazy invention?

1. What is the invention in the text?

   Ⓐ a fork

   Ⓑ a knife

   Ⓒ a spoon

   Ⓓ chopsticks

2. How did the android feel as he looked through the telescope?

   Ⓐ sad

   Ⓑ bored

   Ⓒ confused

   Ⓓ angry

3. How do you know the text is fiction?

   _____

   _____

4. What is something the humans could have been eating?

   _____

   _____

Name: _____ Date: _____

 **As You Read**

Circle words or phrases that are descriptive.

Into the Future

The terrain on the planet was rocky. The robots did their best to cross the field. They were trying to settle into their new home. Problems with another robot nation had caused these robots to flee.

The robots had their own language. Their language did not sound like any human language. They used clicks and other noises that sounded like machines. The robots organized and created their command center. They thought they were ready for anything.

But the robots did not know something. They were not alone! On the other side of the field was a large hill. And an army of creatures was headed right for them. The body of each creature was covered in spikes instead of hair. Every creature had four ears and six arms. They were unlike any other creatures in the universe.

The creatures came over the hill. The robots were not prepared. The creatures were twice as big as them! They were also twice as strong. They were ready for war. The robots and the creatures fought. It went on day and night.

In the end, the robots were badly defeated. The robots who were left flew away. They went to find their next home.

Directions: Read "Into the Future." Then, answer the questions.

1. Which shows a strong connection to this text?

   (A) I have fights with my brothers and go to another room to get away.

   (B) I was Superman for Halloween.

   (C) My dad is the tallest in our family.

   (D) The field at school was rocky before the grass was planted.

2. Which best summarizes the text?

   (A) The robots cannot win so they hide and do not fight.

   (B) The robots can fly anywhere.

   (C) The robots talk in many languages.

   (D) The robots are still on the move, after being defeated by creatures.

3. What is a problem in the text?

   (A) The robots fly.   (C) The robots land safely.

   (B) The robots need a new   (D) The planet is rocky.
       home.

4. Which best describes the robot language?

   (A) There is no language.   (C) It sounds like English.

   (B) It sounds like machines.   (D) It is sign language.

5. Describe the problem and solution in the story.

Problem	Solution

Name: _____ **Date:** _____

Directions: Reread "Into the Future." Then, respond to the prompt.

Write a new ending for this story. Change it or add to it to make it different. Draw a picture to go with your writing.

_____

_____

_____

_____

_____

_____

_____

_____

_____

_____

_____

135044—180 Days of Reading

© Shell Education

Welcome Back!

Found in Central Park

Did you lose a robot dog? This one was found near the large fountain. I know someone must miss it.

Get in touch at (555)-725-8990. Describe the dog to me. That is how I'll know it belongs to you. Then you can have it back!

Name: _____ Date: _____

Directions: Read "Found in Central Park." Then, answer the questions.

1. Where was the robot dog found?
   - (A) at the zoo
   - (B) near the fountain
   - (C) up in a tree
   - (D) at the playground

2. Which words have the opposite meaning?
   - (A) *near* and *close*
   - (B) *love* and *miss*
   - (C) *lost* and *found*
   - (D) *dog* and *puppy*

3. What does the listing say to do after calling the number?
   - (A) Go to the large fountain.
   - (B) Describe the dog.
   - (C) Come and get the dog.
   - (D) Wait until the next day to get it.

4. What is a synonym for the word *large*?
   - (A) huge
   - (B) little
   - (C) small
   - (D) mini

5. Why doesn't the author use a picture of the robot dog on the listing?

   _____

   _____

   _____

   _____

Name: _____ **Date:** _____

Directions: Closely read these texts. Then, study the listing on page 131. Look for two-syllable words in each text. Write the words in the chart.

Close-Reading Texts

The Mars Rovers	Into the Future
There are even robots in space! Five rovers are on Mars. Rovers are robotic vehicles. They move around and take pictures. They carry tools to study rocks, wind, and weather. They help people learn about Mars.	The robots organized and created their command center. They thought they were ready for anything.

But the robots did not know something. They were not alone! On the other side of the field was a large hill. And an army of creatures was headed right for them. |

Text	Two-Syllable Words
The Mars Rovers	
Into the Future	
Found in Central Park	

Name: _____ Date: _____

Directions: Closely read these texts. Then, write about the authors' purpose for each of these texts.

Close-Reading Texts

The Mars Rovers	Into the Future
The first rover landed in 1997. It found information about the environment. It found that Mars was not always cold and dry. It was once warm and wet. Two more rovers arrived six years later. They learned about the past. Mars used to have lakes. It had rivers.	The creatures came over the hill. The robots were not prepared. The creatures were twice as big as them! They were also twice as strong. They were ready for war. The robots and the creatures fought. It went on day and night. In the end, the robots were badly defeated. The robots who were left flew away. They went to find their next home.

Authors' Purpose

Why did the author write the text? What do they want readers to know or learn? How do they want readers to feel?

The Mars Rovers	Into the Future
_____	_____
_____	_____
_____	_____
_____	_____
_____	_____

Name: _____ **Date:** _____

Directions: Think about the texts from this unit. Then, respond to the prompt.

If you could invent any type of robot, what would it be? Describe it. What will it do? What problem will it solve for you or for others? What does it look like? Draw a picture of it.

_____

_____

_____

_____

_____

_____

_____

_____

_____

Name: _____ **Date:** _____

Directions: Think about your robot invention from page 135. Then, pretend you lost your robot. Make a poster about your lost robot. Tell where you lost it and why you want it back.

Directions: Read the text, then answer the questions.

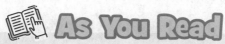 As You Read

Underline information that is new or interesting to you.

The Famous Eiffel Tower

Have you ever heard of the Eiffel Tower? It is a famous building. It is in Paris, France. It is a beautiful monument. It was built in 1889. It took more than two years to build it! Many visitors go to the tower each year. It lights up at night. What a sight!

1. Which sentence best summarizes the text?
   - Ⓐ The Eiffel Tower gets many visitors.
   - Ⓑ The Eiffel Tower lights up at night.
   - Ⓒ The Eiffel Tower is a famous building in Paris.
   - Ⓓ The Eiffel Tower took two years to build.

2. Which statement is **not** true about the Eiffel Tower?
   - Ⓐ It took less than two years to build.
   - Ⓑ It is a famous building.
   - Ⓒ It is in Paris, France.
   - Ⓓ It was built in 1889.

3. Which words have the same vowel sound?
   - Ⓐ *two* and *tower*
   - Ⓑ *lights* and *sight*
   - Ⓒ *took* and *more*
   - Ⓓ *heard* and *each*

4. What is another term for *monument*?
   - Ⓐ bright light
   - Ⓑ famous building
   - Ⓒ French
   - Ⓓ street

Name: _____   Date: _____

Directions: Read the text, then answer the questions.

Put a ☆ next to information you already knew.

Money Everywhere

People can buy things with money. They shop for what they need. They use bills and coins to pay. This is true in places around the world. Most countries have their own type of money. Dollars are used in the United States. Euros are used in parts of Europe. People who travel have to exchange money. They must use the money of the country they are visiting.

1. What is the text mostly about?
   - (A) the dollar bill
   - (B) types of money
   - (C) euros
   - (D) shopping

2. Which type of money is used in Europe?
   - (A) a euro
   - (B) a bill
   - (C) a coin
   - (D) money

3. Which statement is true based on the text?
   - (A) All countries use the same money.
   - (B) People can use dollars everywhere.
   - (C) People who travel have to exchange money.
   - (D) People use their own money everywhere.

4. Which is **not** a word that has to do with money?
   - (A) spent
   - (B) shop
   - (C) buy
   - (D) places

   135044—180 Days of Reading

Name: _____ **Date:** _____

Directions: Read the text, then answer the questions.

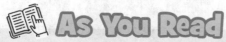 **As You Read**

Put a ☆ next to information you already knew.

Continents of the World

Earth has oceans and continents. Continents are large areas of land. There are seven of them in the world. They are all different sizes. They are all different shapes, too. Continents can have many countries. They may have dozens. Some of them have just a few. One continent has only one country. Which one is it? It is Australia.

1. What statement below is **not** true about continents?

   Ⓐ They are large areas of land.

   Ⓑ Australia is one of the continents of the world.

   Ⓒ They may be divided into smaller countries.

   Ⓓ There are eight of them.

2. Which has the same root word as *divided*?

   Ⓐ video

   Ⓑ division

   Ⓒ vice

   Ⓓ dive

3. What is unique about Australia?

   _____

   _____

4. How could you learn more about continents?

   _____

   _____

 **As You Read**

Put a ☆ next to reasons you might want to visit France.

France

France is a country. It is in Europe. It is a beautiful part of the world. France is one of the oldest nations. Evidence shows humans settled there more than 16,000 years ago!

The landscape is very diverse. There are warm beaches in the south. They are found on the Mediterranean Sea. The French Riviera is there. It is famous for its beaches. The country also has huge mountains. They are the French Alps. France has a lot of land for growing crops, too. The country makes many food items. A lot of these are shipped around the world. France is famous for wine and cheese products.

Many people want to visit France. It is a popular place! About 75 million people visit every year. They love the beaches. They visit the mountains. They also flock to Paris. This is the capital city. People like to walk around the beautiful city. They enjoy the sights. They shop and eat. They visit museums. They see the Eiffel Tower.

You might visit France one day. If you do, try to learn a few words in French. Then, you can talk to people there. Start with *bonjour* and *au revoir*. This way, you can say hello and goodbye!

Directions: Read "France." Then, answer the questions.

1. Which statement shows a strong connection to the text?
   - (A) Cheese makes my stomach hurt.
   - (B) My family goes on trips, and we learn about places we visit.
   - (C) I like to swim and play at the beach.
   - (D) I can say a few words in Spanish.

2. What is France famous for?
   - (A) only wine
   - (B) only cheese
   - (C) wine and cheese
   - (D) steak

3. What does *flock* mean in the third paragraph?
   - (A) a group of birds
   - (B) visit in large numbers
   - (C) fake snow
   - (D) to leave

4. Which part of French life is **not** in the text?
   - (A) its tourism
   - (B) its landscape
   - (C) its history
   - (D) its government

5. Write the main idea of the text. Then, write three details.

Main Idea		
Detail	**Detail**	**Detail**

Name: _____ **Date:** _____

Directions: Reread "France." Then, respond to the prompt.

Think about all that you have learned about France. What do you think is the most interesting thing about France? Describe it. Explain your thinking. Draw a picture to go with your writing.

_____

_____

_____

_____

_____

_____

_____

_____

_____

_____

Directions: Read the text, then answer the questions.

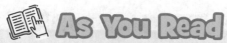 **As You Read**

Circle words with long vowel sounds.

Anywhere in the World

Olivia's friend, Charlotte, was excited. Her family was going to Disneyland for fall break! After school, Olivia told her parents.

"I wish I could go," she said. "It sounds like so much fun."

"Don't worry. We'll have fun at home," Mom answered.

Olivia didn't think staying home sounded fun. Then, Dad got the globe.

"Spin it," he said. "We can go anywhere in the world."

Olivia put her finger on the globe. She gave it a spin. It stopped with her finger on France.

"We're going to France for vacation?" she asked.

1. Which word is **not** a compound word?
   - (A) Disneyland
   - (B) anywhere
   - (C) family
   - (D) outside

2. What does Dad get?
   - (A) money
   - (B) the globe
   - (C) his wallet
   - (D) a drink of water

3. Where does Olivia's finger land?
   - (A) France
   - (B) Germany
   - (C) United States
   - (D) Spain

4. What is the past tense form of *spin*?
   - (A) spinned
   - (B) spun
   - (C) spins
   - (D) spinning

Name: _____ Date: _____

Directions: Read the text, then answer the questions.

Draw a ☆ whenever you identify a new character.

Learning the Language

Olivia was puzzled. How would they be able to get plane tickets on such short notice?

"We don't need to," her mother said. "We can bring France to us!"

"How?" Olivia asked. She still wasn't sure this idea sounded fun.

"First, we need to learn the language," Dad said. "Do you know how to say 'hello' in French?"

Olivia shook her head. Dad opened his laptop, and together, they learned some French words.

"*Bonjour*," Dad said. "That means 'hello.'"

Olivia tried, too.

"*Bien*," she said, "means 'good.'"

1. Which word *best* describes Olivia's family?
   - (A) traveling
   - (B) sad
   - (C) curious
   - (D) tired

2. What does *bonjour* mean in French?
   - (A) hello
   - (B) goodbye
   - (C) welcome
   - (D) see you later

3. Which word has more than two syllables?
   - (A) afford
   - (B) mother
   - (C) computer
   - (D) France

4. Which word means the opposite of *open*?
   - (A) touched
   - (B) closed
   - (C) said
   - (D) saw

Name: _____ **Date:** _____

Directions: Read the text, then answer the questions.

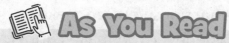 **As You Read**

Draw a rectangle around new or interesting words.

All About France

The next day, Dad said, "There's a lot to see in France. I'd like to visit the Eiffel Tower."

Mom agreed. "Let's go to museums too," she said.

Olivia remembered something. "Isn't there a famous painting in Paris? I think it's called the *Mona Lisa*," she said.

"I think you're right," Mom said. "Let's find out!"

After doing research online, they settled on the couch to watch a movie. It was all about France.

---

1. What does mom want to visit in France?

   (A) the Eiffel Tower

   (B) the museums

   (C) the Mona Lisa painting

   (D) the movie theater

2. What is the plural form of *couch*?

   (A) couchs

   (B) couchies

   (C) couches

   (D) couch

3. Where is the family getting their information from?

_____

4. What else would you like to learn about France?

_____

_____

 **As You Read**

Think of connections you can make to the text.
Write a ∞ whenever you make connections.

A Delicious Vacation

Seeing the sights of France was exciting. When the movie was over, everyone was hungry.

"Why don't we go to a nice French restaurant?" Mom suggested. She led the family into the kitchen.

"Welcome to Café Miller," Mom said. "We can make our own French food here."

Olivia looked doubtful. "Do we have the right ingredients?" she asked.

Dad grinned at her. He pointed to a long loaf of bread on the counter.

"This is a baguette," Dad said. He cut it into slices. Then, he spread soft brie cheese on top. It was delicious!

"What else can I try?" Olivia asked.

Her mother made crepes. They were like very thin pancakes. She folded them and put berries inside. Olivia liked those too.

"I hope you left room for dessert," Mom said. She opened a bakery box. Inside, Olivia saw brightly colored circles. They looked like cookie sandwiches.

"These are called *macarons*. They're a French dessert," Mom told her.

Olivia tried one. It tasted amazing! It was very light and tasted like lemon.

"How do you like our vacation so far?" Dad asked.

Olivia smiled. "It is very *bien*!" she said.

Directions: Read "A Delicious Vacation." Then, answer the questions.

1. Which French food does the family **not** try?

A   crepes

B   French onion soup

C   macaroons

D   baguette

2. Who spreads the cheese on the bread?

A   Mom

B   Dad

C   Olivia

D   nobody

3. Which word best describes how Olivia is feeling now?

A   upset

B   confused

C   joyful

D   content

4. Which word has the same vowel sound as the word *cheese*?

A   fold

B   bread

C   macaroon

D   eat

5. Write a different French food the family tries in each box.

French Food

Name: _____ **Date:** _____

Directions: Reread "A Delicious Vacation." Then, respond to the prompt.

So far, Olivia's family tried a few different French foods. They practiced some of the language. They found a few major landmarks. Write the next part of the story. Give details about what they will do, see, or learn next.

_____

_____

_____

_____

_____

_____

_____

_____

_____

_____

_____

Les Desserts

Menu

Tarte Tatin
A sweet apple pastry

Crème Caramel
Custard topped with caramel

Éclair
A cream-filled pastry

Dame Blanche
Vanilla ice cream with warm chocolate sauce

Name: _____   Date: _____

Directions: Read "Les Desserts." Then, answer the questions.

1. Which dessert includes ice cream?
   - (A) Tarte Tatin
   - (B) Crème Caramel
   - (C) Éclair
   - (D) Dame Blanche

2. What is the éclair filled with?
   - (A) ice cream
   - (B) chocolate
   - (C) cream
   - (D) apples

3. Which word has more than two syllables?
   - (A) apple
   - (B) vanilla
   - (C) pastry
   - (D) sauce

4. Which dessert is made with a fruit?
   - (A) Tarte Tatin
   - (B) Crème Caramel
   - (C) Éclair
   - (D) Dame Blanche

5. Which dessert would you order from this menu? Explain why it would be the best.

   _____

   _____

   _____

   _____

   _____

   _____

   _____

Name: _____   Date: _____

Directions: Closely read these texts. Then, study the menu on page 149. Look for nouns. Write the nouns in the chart.

Close-Reading Texts

France	A Delicious Vacation
France is a country. It is in Europe. It is a beautiful part of the world. France is one of the oldest nations. Evidence shows humans settled there more than 16,000 years ago! The landscape is very diverse. There are warm beaches in the south. They are found on the Mediterranean Sea.	Seeing the sights of France was exciting. When the movie was over, everyone was hungry. "Why don't we go to a nice French restaurant?" Mom suggested. She led the family into the kitchen. "Welcome to Café Miller," Mom said. "We can make our own French food here."

Text	Nouns (Common and Proper)
France	
A Delicious Vacation	
Les Desserts	

Name: _____   Date: _____

Directions: Closely read these texts. Then, compare the content of the two texts.

Close-Reading Texts

France	A Delicious Vacation
Many people want to visit France. It is a popular place! About 75 million people visit every year. They love the beaches. They visit the mountains. They also flock to Paris. This is the capital city. People like to walk around the beautiful city. They enjoy the sights. They shop and eat. They visit museums. They see the Eiffel Tower.	"I hope you left room for dessert," Mom said. She opened a bakery box. Inside, Olivia saw brightly colored circles. They looked like cookie sandwiches. "These are called *macarons*. They're a French dessert," Mom told her. Olivia tried one. It tasted amazing! It was very light and tasted like lemon. "How do you like our vacation so far?" Dad asked. Olivia smiled. "It is very *bien*!" she said.

France

Both   **A Delicious Vacation**

Name: _____ **Date:** _____

Directions: Think about the texts from this unit. Then, respond to the prompt.

You have a pen pal in Paris, France. This pen pal knows nothing about where you're from. Write them a letter. Teach them a few things about where you're from. Then, ask questions you have about France.

_____

_____ ,

_____

_____

_____

_____

_____

_____

_____

_____

_____ ,

_____

Name: _____ **Date:** _____

Directions: Design a menu of your own. Include at least one appetizer, one main dish, and one dessert. Draw pictures of at least one item on your menu. Don't forget to put prices. Write a brief description of each item.

Name: _____   Date: _____

Directions: Read the text, then answer the questions.

 As You Read

Underline information that is new or interesting to you.

Old-Fashioned Toys

Children have always had toys. But toys have changed over time. Pioneer children played differently. Many of their toys were homemade. They used sticks to make wooden hoops. They had dolls made of corn husks. They made button spinners out of buttons and string.

1. What were dolls made of?
   - (A) sticks
   - (B) corn husks
   - (C) buttons
   - (D) string

2. What toy is **not** mentioned in the text?
   - (A) dolls
   - (B) wooden hoops
   - (C) toy cars
   - (D) button spinners

3. Which word from the text is a compound word?
   - (A) children
   - (B) wooden
   - (C) spinners
   - (D) homemade

4. What is the main idea of this text?
   - (A) Children like toys.
   - (B) Toys have changed over time.
   - (C) They used sticks to make hoops.
   - (D) Many toys were homemade.

Name: _____ Date: _____

Directions: Read the text, then answer the questions.

 **As You Read**

Put a ☆ next to information you already knew.

Modern Toys

Many modern toys are high-tech. They have screens and make sounds. Kids use them to play video games. They watch shows. They listen to music, and they dance and sing along. Kids can also use high-tech toys to make games, shows, and music of their own.

1. What kids' activity is **not** mentioned?

   (A) video games

   (B) watching shows

   (C) listening to music

   (D) writing a story

2. Which word has the opposite meaning of *modern*?

   (A) new

   (B) old-fashioned

   (C) fancy

   (D) high-tech

3. What is the plural form of the word *watch*?

   (A) watches

   (B) watching

   (C) watched

   (D) watchs

4. Which word has more than one syllable?

   (A) screens

   (B) sounds

   (C) games

   (D) modern

Name: _____   **Date:** _____

Directions: Read the text, then answer the questions.

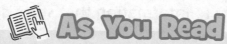

Write a **?** wherever you have a question about the text.

Timeless Toys

Old-fashioned toys can be fun. Many are still popular today. Do you like Lego® blocks? Have you ever played with Play-Doh®? Do you like to shake your Magic 8 Ball® and learn what the future holds? These toys were invented long ago.

1. What is another word for *popular*?

    Ⓐ liked   Ⓒ unpopular

    Ⓑ disliked   Ⓓ old-fashioned

2. Which word is **not** a verb?

    Ⓐ play   Ⓒ toys

    Ⓑ shake   Ⓓ learn

3. What is one question you would ask a Magic 8 Ball?

_____

_____

4. What is your favorite toy from the text? Tell why.

_____

_____

_____

 **As You Read**

Put an **!** next to information that surprises you.

An Accidental Invention

Silly Putty® is a strange toy. It comes in a plastic egg. It's squishy and stretchy. It feels like gum or a ball of goo.

James Wright made Silly Putty in 1943. He was trying to make a substitute for rubber. But it did not work out. His invention was an accident!

Someone else saw a better use for it. Peter Hodgson sold Silly Putty as a toy. It caught on fast. Kids all over the world loved playing with it. They bounced it. They stretched it. They used it to copy their comic book pictures.

Today, Silly Putty is more than a toy. It has all kinds of practical uses. People use it to pick up dirt. Athletes squeeze it to train their muscles. Astronauts have used it in space. It can hold their tools in place.

Kids still love Silly Putty, too. It's a toy that sells millions each year.

Directions: Read "An Accidental Invention." Then, answer the questions.

1. What is Silly Putty compared to?
   - Ⓐ candy
   - Ⓑ gum
   - Ⓒ an egg
   - Ⓓ food

2. What is Silly Putty **not** used for?
   - Ⓐ stretching
   - Ⓑ bouncing
   - Ⓒ eating
   - Ⓓ squeezing

3. Who uses Silly Putty?
   - Ⓐ kids only
   - Ⓑ adults only
   - Ⓒ kids and adults
   - Ⓓ animals

4. What do astronauts use Silly Putty for?
   - Ⓐ picking up dirt
   - Ⓑ training muscles
   - Ⓒ playing with it
   - Ⓓ holding tools in place

5. Write the uses for Silly Putty in the boxes.

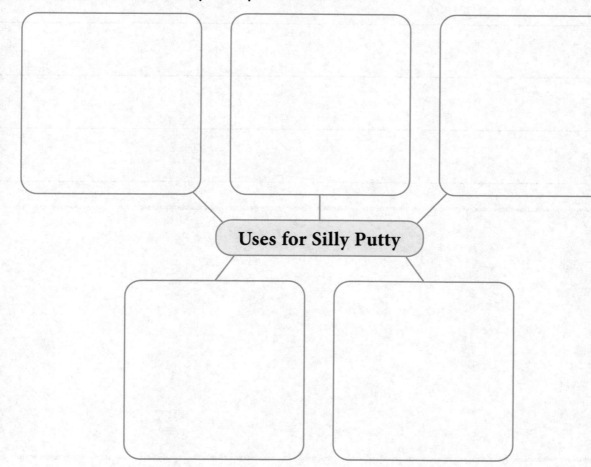

Uses for Silly Putty

Name: _____ **Date:** _____

Directions: Reread "An Accidental Invention." Then, respond to the prompt.

What would you use Silly Putty for? For play, something more useful, or maybe both? Give details about how you would use it. Draw a picture to go with your writing.

_____

_____

_____

_____

_____

_____

_____

Directions: Read the text, then answer the questions.

 **As You Read**

Make predictions about what you think will happen next.

Game Time

Jazmine, Elsie, Colton, and Ari met in Jazmine's backyard.

"We have an hour until dinner time," Ari said. "Want to play soccer?"

Colton frowned. "It's too hot to run around, so I'd rather play a board game."

"I don't know," Elsie objected. "Board games make me feel bored."

The group laughed. But they still couldn't agree on what to do with their time.

"I like pretend games," Jazmine said. "Can't we play make-believe?"

1. What does Colton want to play?

- (A) soccer
- (B) a board game
- (C) make-believe
- (D) nothing

2. What context clue helps you understand how Colton feels about playing soccer?

- (A) He frowned.
- (B) He smiled.
- (C) He cheered.
- (D) He laughed.

3. Whose backyard are they in?

- (A) Elsie's
- (B) Jazmine's
- (C) Colton's
- (D) Ari's

4. What does *objected* mean in this text?

- (A) agreed
- (B) shouted
- (C) disagreed
- (D) yelled

Name: _____   Date: _____

Directions: Read the text, and answer the questions.

As You Read

Think of connections you can make to the text.
Write a ∞ whenever you make connections.

A New Way to Play

Fifteen minutes went by. The kids kept arguing. They couldn't agree on what to play.

"We're wasting all our time," Colton said. "We should just pick something."

"But we have to agree on it. Otherwise, it isn't fair," Ari said.

"How about we make up a new game?" Elsie suggested.

Jazmine looked excited. "We should include something from each of the different games we like!" she said.

1. Who says they must all agree on the game?
  - Ⓐ Colton
  - Ⓑ Jazmine
  - Ⓒ Ari
  - Ⓓ Elsie

2. Which word means the opposite of *excited*?
  - Ⓐ happy
  - Ⓑ bored
  - Ⓒ thrilled
  - Ⓓ intrigued

3. Why are the kids arguing?
  - Ⓐ They are upset with each other.
  - Ⓑ They can't agree on a game to play.
  - Ⓒ Someone says something rude.
  - Ⓓ They are excited.

4. Which word is **not** in past tense?
  - Ⓐ agree
  - Ⓑ argued
  - Ⓒ made
  - Ⓓ included

Name: _____ Date: _____

Directions: Read the text, and answer the questions.

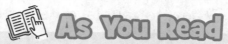

Make predictions about what you think will happen next.

Playing Without a Plan

The kids started talking about how to make their new game. Then, another friend of theirs showed up.

"Can I play, too?" Katy asked. "How do you play?"

Everyone looked at each other. No one knew how to answer, and they didn't want to waste any more time on planning.

"Let's just start playing," Jazmine said. "We can figure it out as we go."

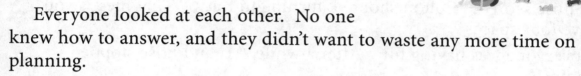

1. Who is the new friend that joined?
   (A) Elsie
   (B) Jazmine
   (C) Katy
   (D) Colton

2. What is the past tense spelling of the word *plan*?
   (A) planns
   (B) planned
   (C) planing
   (D) planed

3. Why does everyone look at each other when Katy asks how to play?

   _____

   _____

4. How would you feel if you were Katy?

   _____

   _____

As You Read

Draw a ♡ next to your favorite part(s).

Making Rules for a Made-Up Game

Jazmine liked the new game right from the start. She decided to pretend she was a talking parrot. Her parrot's name was Polly. "Caw, caw, Polly wants a cracker!" she croaked in the middle of the yard. She flapped her arms, pretending they were wings.

Ari and Elise ran around her, kicking the soccer ball.

Colton sat on the sidelines with Katy. They had a board game open on the ground.

"Elise scored!" Colton shouted, turning to Katy. "That means you move four spaces."

Everyone was having fun. After a while, Ari and Elise stopped running.

"The game is over," Elise announced, happily. "I scored the most points, so I won!"

The other kids clapped. Then Jazmine cawed again, and Colton rolled the dice.

"What are you doing?" Ari asked. "We finished the game."

Katy looked puzzled. "You finished the soccer game. But we didn't finish our board game," she said.

"That doesn't matter. It was all part of the same game," Elise argued. "And now it's over because I won."

Jazmine shook her head. "Nobody wins. That wouldn't be fair. How could I win at pretending?" she asked.

The kids fell silent. Then, Colton had an idea. "We made up a game we like, so why don't we make up rules we like too?" he said.

Just then Jazmine's mom called, "Dinner time!"

"I have one," Jazmine suggested, quickly. "We can change the rules if we don't like them."

Everyone laughed.

"Perfect," Elise agreed. "Let's meet tomorrow and play again!"

Directions: Read "Making Rules for a Made-Up Game." Then, answer the questions.

1. Who pretends to be a talking parrot?
   - (A) Katy
   - (B) Jazmine
   - (C) Colton
   - (D) Elsie

2. What does the phrase *Katy looked puzzled* mean?
   - (A) She was happy.
   - (B) She was tired.
   - (C) She was confused.
   - (D) She was upset.

3. Who is playing a board game?
   - (A) Colton and Katy
   - (B) Jazmine and Elise
   - (C) Katy and Ari
   - (D) Ari and Elise

4. Why do they stop playing?
   - (A) They are too upset.
   - (B) It is time for dinner.
   - (C) They lose the soccer ball.
   - (D) Someone gets hurt.

5. Write the problem and solution in the story.

Problem	Solution

Name: _____ **Date:** _____

Directions: Reread "Making Rules for a Made-Up Game." Then, respond to the prompt.

Think about the rules to the made-up game. What rule would you change, if any? What rule would you add? Tell why.

_____

_____

_____

_____

_____

_____

_____

_____

_____

_____

How to Play

TV Tag Game Instructions

1. Choose a player to be "it."

2. All players scatter while "it" closes their eyes and counts to 10.

3. "It" tries to tag the other players. If tagged, that player becomes "it."

4. Players can avoid being tagged by calling out a TV show and squatting on the ground.

Name: _____ **Date:** _____

Directions: Read "How to Play." Then, answer the questions.

1. Which two words have the same vowel sound?

   (A) *choose* and *close*

   (B) *players* and *tagged*

   (C) *scatter* and *tag*

   (D) *show* and *ground*

2. Which step involves closing your eyes?

   (A) step 1

   (B) step 2

   (C) step 3

   (D) step 4

3. What do you do after calling out a TV show?

   (A) chase another player

   (B) become "it"

   (C) sit out of that round

   (D) squat on the ground

4. What number do you count to if you're "it"?

   (A) 10

   (B) 20

   (C) 30

   (D) 100

5. If you could add or change one step to these instructions, what would it be? Why?

   _____

   _____

   _____

   _____

   _____

   _____

   _____

Name: _____ **Date:** _____

Directions: Closely read these texts. Then, study the instruction sheet on page 167. Look for two-syllable words in each text. Write the words in the chart.

Close-Reading Texts

An Accidental Invention	Making Rules for a Made-Up Game
Silly Putty is a strange toy. It comes in a plastic egg. It's squishy and stretchy. It feels like gum or a ball of goo. James Wright made Silly Putty in 1943. He was trying to make a substitute for rubber. But it did not work out. His invention was an accident!	Jazmine liked the new game right from the start. She decided to pretend she was a talking parrot. Her parrot's name was Polly. "Caw, caw, Polly wants a cracker!" she croaked in the middle of the yard. She flapped her arms, pretending they were wings. Ari and Elise ran around her, kicking the soccer ball. Colton sat on the sidelines with Katy. They had a board game open on the ground.

Text	Two-Syllable Words
An Accidental Invention	
Making Rules for a Made-Up Game	
How to Play	

Name: _____ Date: _____

Directions: Closely read these texts. Then, write the authors' purpose for each of these texts.

Close-Reading Texts

An Accidental Invention	Making Rules for a Made-Up Game
Today, Silly Putty is more than a toy. It has all kinds of practical uses. People use it to pick up dirt. Athletes squeeze it to train their muscles. Astronauts have used it in space. It can hold their tools in place. Kids still love Silly Putty, too. It's a toy that sells millions each year.	The kids fell silent. Then, Colton had an idea. "We made up a game we like, so why don't we make up rules we like too?" he said. Just then Jazmine's mom called, "Dinner time!" "I have one," Jazmine suggested, quickly. "We can change the rules if we don't like them." Everyone laughed.

Authors' Purpose

Why did the author write the text? What do they want readers to know or learn? How do they want readers to feel?

An Accidental Invention	Making Rules for a Made-Up Game
_____ _____ _____ _____	_____ _____ _____ _____

Name: _____ **Date:** _____

Directions: Think about the texts from this unit. Then, respond to the prompt.

Think of a time you created something by accident. What was it? Did you like it? Was it fun or useful? Maybe it was food, a game, or even an art piece. Describe what you made and how you made it.

_____

_____

_____

_____

_____

_____

_____

_____

_____

_____

_____

Name: _____ **Date:** _____

Directions: Make up your own game. Think about what rules and steps are needed. Make an instruction sheet for others to follow.

Name: _____ **Date:** _____

Directions: Read the text, then answer the questions.

As You Read

Draw a rectangle around new or important vocabulary words.

Space Sleeping

Sleeping in space can be tricky. In space, there is no gravity. Astronauts float around at space stations. But crew members still have to sleep. So, space stations have private rooms for sleeping. The crew members are anchored to their beds. This way, they can stay in their beds and sleep peacefully.

1. What is the text mostly about?
   - (A) space
   - (B) sleeping in space
   - (C) sleeping
   - (D) the space station

2. Which is another meaning of the word *anchored*?
   - (A) floated
   - (B) attached
   - (C) tucked in
   - (D) glued

3. Which word has the same suffix as *sleeping*?
   - (A) ping
   - (B) sleet
   - (C) string
   - (D) talking

4. How do astronauts sleep in space?
   - (A) They are attached to a bed.
   - (B) They float around.
   - (C) They don't sleep.
   - (D) They all sleep in the same room.

Name: _____ **Date:** _____

Directions: Read the text, then answer the questions.

Underline information that is new or interesting to you.

Comets

A comet is a small object that can be found in the solar system. A comet is a mix of ice, dust, and small rocks. It has a long tail. The tail is made up of gas and dust particles. It can have a fuzzy outline called a *coma*. This can be seen when the comet gets close to the sun.

Halley's Comet might be the most famous comet. It can be seen from Earth about every 76 years.

1. What is this text mostly about?
   - (A) Halley's Comet
   - (B) comets
   - (C) the solar system
   - (D) the sun

2. When can a comet's fuzzy outline be seen?
   - (A) when it explodes
   - (B) when it gets close to the sun
   - (C) every seventy-six years
   - (D) when it stops moving

3. Which is a compound word?
   - (A) comet
   - (B) solar
   - (C) outline
   - (D) fuzzy

4. What does *tail* mean in this text?
   - (A) back of a coin
   - (B) rear part of an animal's body
   - (C) the start of something
   - (D) stream of gas and dust particles

Directions: Read the text, then answer the questions.

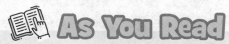

Put a ☆ next to information you already knew.

Planets

There used to be nine planets in the solar system. Pluto was the ninth planet. Today, Pluto is not considered a planet. It is known as a dwarf planet. It still orbits the sun like the other eight planets. But it is much smaller.

1. What does this text tell you about Pluto?

   Ⓐ Pluto is a dwarf planet.

   Ⓑ Pluto is not a dwarf planet.

   Ⓒ Pluto used to be a dwarf planet.

   Ⓓ Pluto is the largest dwarf planet.

2. Which is a proper noun?

   Ⓐ planets

   Ⓑ Pluto

   Ⓒ today

   Ⓓ there

3. What makes Pluto similar to the eight planets?

   _____

   _____

4. What do you think *orbit* means? Use the image to help you.

   _____

   _____

Name: _____ Date: _____

As You Read

Draw a ⸮ anywhere you have questions or want to know more.

Inside the Space Station

The International Space Station is like a city in space. People from 16 different countries helped build it. Astronauts live there. They study space. They want to know how humans can live away from Earth. A crew always stays on the space station. The crew rotates. Up to six people can be there at once. This gives many astronauts a turn to visit.

Crew members have to get creative for their meals. They do not have a refrigerator or a stove. They just have a food warmer for cans. Astronauts used to eat only freeze-dried food. They would add water to it and have a meal. Now, their meals look more like what people eat on Earth. They keep their food on a special tray. This helps keep the food from floating away.

Astronauts need to stay healthy on the space station. They work hard while they are up there. Rest is very important. Crew members have private places to sleep. Exercise is important, too. Muscles and bones can grow weak in space. So, astronauts must stay fit. They may use equipment to make sure their bodies stay healthy. Life on the space station sure is interesting!

Directions: Read "Inside the Space Station." Then, answer the questions.

1. Which gives the best summary of the text?

   Ⓐ The space station is like a city in space, and astronauts study life in space.

   Ⓑ The space station was built by people from around the world.

   Ⓒ Astronauts can eat regular food on the space station.

   Ⓓ Astronauts must exercise and stay healthy.

2. Which definition of *fit* is used in the fourth paragraph?

   Ⓐ appropriate

   Ⓑ tantrum

   Ⓒ correct size

   Ⓓ strong and healthy

3. Which topic is **not** covered about life on the space station?

   Ⓐ sleeping

   Ⓑ exercising

   Ⓒ eating

   Ⓓ chores

4. Which of the following is true?

   Ⓐ Crew members all sleep in the same room.

   Ⓑ Muscles and bones can get weak in space.

   Ⓒ Astronauts store their food in a refrigerator.

   Ⓓ Eight people can be in the International Space station.

5. Write the main idea of the text. Write three details.

Main Idea

Detail	Detail	Detail

Name: _____ **Date:** _____

Directions: Reread "Inside the Space Station." Then, respond to the prompt.

Think about what life is like on the space station. Would you want to live on the space station? Explain why or why not.

_____

_____

_____

_____

_____

_____

_____

_____

_____

_____

_____

_____

_____

Directions: Read the text, and answer the questions.

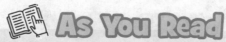

Write an **S** next to words or phrases that tell you about the setting.

Racing to Space

It was movie night at school. When the film was finished, everyone ran to the playground. Silas and Mariana raced to the swings.

Mariana pumped her legs hard. "Look how high I'm going!" she shouted.

Silas tried to go just as high. He looked up at the dark sky where all the stars were shining.

"I'm going to swing into space!" he cried.

1. Which word does **not** have a suffix?
   - Ⓐ going
   - Ⓑ swing
   - Ⓒ shining
   - Ⓓ pumping

2. What do the kids do right after the movie finishes?
   - Ⓐ They pump their legs.
   - Ⓑ They clean up their trash.
   - Ⓒ They run to the playground.
   - Ⓓ They look up at the sky.

3. What is the root word of *shining*?
   - Ⓐ shine
   - Ⓑ shin
   - Ⓒ hine
   - Ⓓ ing

4. What is the setting?
   - Ⓐ space
   - Ⓑ movie theater
   - Ⓒ school
   - Ⓓ park

Name: _____   Date: _____

Directions: Read the text, and answer the questions.

 **As You Read**

Draw an 👁 next to words that help you visualize the story.

The Opposite of Gravity

Silas couldn't believe how high he was swinging. He had never gone that high before.

"I can see over the top of the school," he said.

"Me too," she said. "Something weird is happening. I'm going higher and higher."

Suddenly, both kids felt themselves floating. They were being pulled up. They were moving toward the stars.

"There's a force up here!" Silas said. "It's the opposite of gravity!"

1. Which word has the same vowel sound as in *high*?

- (A) swing
- (B) kids
- (C) I'm
- (D) both

2. What is the weirdest thing that happens?

- (A) They can see over the top of the school.
- (B) They go higher and higher toward space.
- (C) They watch a movie at school.
- (D) They are being pulled down to the ground.

3. Which word means the opposite of *higher*?

- (A) upper
- (B) lower
- (C) longer
- (D) shorter

4. Where are the kids going when they say *there's a force*?

- (A) toward the stars
- (B) to a different swing set
- (C) to jump high off the swings
- (D) to watch another movie

Name: _____ **Date:** _____

Directions: Read the text, and answer the questions.

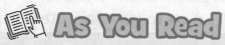

Draw an 👁 next to words that help you visualize the story.

A New Place to Swim

Silas and Mariana floated high up into the sky and looked down. The school appeared very small below them. Then, they couldn't see it at all because they were too high up! Soon, they reached space.

"I can still breathe," Mariana called. "Can you?"

"Yes!" Silas answered. "I can also swim!"

The kids discovered space was like water. They could move through it by pretending they were swimming, but they did not have to hold their breath.

1. What do the kids compare space to?

- Ⓐ sand
- Ⓑ water
- Ⓒ air
- Ⓓ dirt

2. Which word is **not** a real word?

- Ⓐ floated
- Ⓑ answered
- Ⓒ swimmed
- Ⓓ pretended

3. How do the kids move around in space?

_____

_____

4. How would you feel if you were one of the kids in the story?

_____

_____

Draw a ♡ next to your favorite part(s).

Exploring Space

"Look, it's the moon!" Silas said, pointing. "Let's go there first!"

Silas floated on his back. Mariana did the doggy paddle. They swam to the moon and climbed into a giant crater.

"We're weightless!" Mariana said. She bounced along the moon's surface. Silas jumped and floated. He saw something in the stars.

"Saturn!" he shouted. "Let's go there next!"

They crouched down low. They jumped up high and launched into space again. They swam their way over to Saturn. It was a long journey.

"I've always wanted to visit Saturn," Mariana said when they arrived.

She grabbed onto one of Saturn's rings. Silas grabbed it too. The ring began to turn. The kids spun around the planet faster and faster.

"Hold on tight!" Mariana shouted.

But Silas couldn't do it. He let go and shot into space. Mariana didn't want him to go alone. She let go, too. The force of the spinning ring set their speed. They zoomed downward.

"We're leaving space," Silas said. "There's the sky."

They moved lower and lower toward the ground. Then, they were on the swings again.

"Did we just go to space?" Mariana asked.

It all felt like a dream, but they knew it wasn't.

"I think we did!" Silas answered.

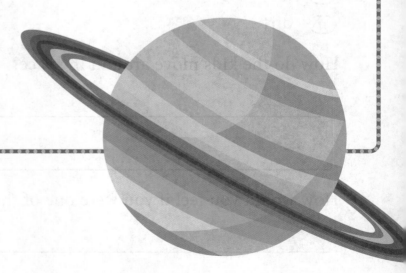

Name: _____ **Date:** _____

Directions: Read "Exploring Space." Then, answer the questions.

1. Where do Silas and Mariana go first?
   - (A) the moon
   - (B) Saturn
   - (C) the sun
   - (D) the swings

2. Why does Mariana shout, *hold on tight*?
   - (A) They are floating away.
   - (B) Saturn's rings are spinning fast.
   - (C) They start lowering to the ground quickly.
   - (D) They don't know what is happening.

3. Which word means *to go quickly*?
   - (A) floated
   - (B) climbed
   - (C) zoomed
   - (D) grabbed

4. What does Silas compare going into space to?
   - (A) sitting near the ocean
   - (B) having a dream
   - (C) swinging on the swings
   - (D) floating in a pool

5. Describe the beginning, middle, and end of the story.

Beginning	Middle	End

Name: _____ **Date:** _____

Directions: Reread "Exploring Space." Then, respond to the prompt.

Imagine you floated into space with Silas and Mariana. What would you want to explore with them? What adventures would you have together? Draw a picture to show your ideas.

_____

_____

_____

_____

_____

_____

_____

Space: A Haiku

Eyes on the dark sky
Bright moon, stars, other planets
Many mysteries

Name: _____ Date: _____

Directions: Read "Space: A Haiku." Then, answer the questions.

1. A haiku is a type of _____.

   (A) narrative

   (B) poem

   (C) short story

   (D) play

2. What is the singular spelling for *mysteries*?

   (A) misty

   (B) mysterie

   (C) mystery

   (D) mysteries

3. How does the haiku describe the sky?

   (A) dark

   (B) bright

   (C) mysterious

   (D) cloudy

4. What is **not** mentioned in the haiku?

   (A) stars

   (B) moon

   (C) planets

   (D) sun

5. Do you think space is mysterious? Why or why not?

_____

_____

_____

_____

_____

_____

Directions: Closely read these texts. Then, study the poem on page 185. Look for words about space in each text. Write the words in the chart.

Close-Reading Texts

Inside the Space Station	Exploring Space
The International Space Station is like a city in space. People from 16 different countries helped build it. Astronauts live there. They study space. They want to know how humans can live away from Earth. A crew always stays on the space station. The crew rotates. Up to six people can be there at once. This gives many astronauts a turn to visit.	"Look, it's the moon!" Silas said, pointing. "Let's go there first!" Silas floated on his back. Mariana did the doggy paddle. They swam to the moon and climbed into a giant crater. "We're weightless!" Mariana said. She bounced along the moon's surface. Silas jumped and floated. He saw something in the stars. "Saturn!" he shouted. "Let's go there next!"

Text	Space Words
Inside the Space Station	
Exploring Space	
Space: A Haiku	

Name: _____   Date: _____

Directions: Closely read these texts. Then, draw the setting of each text.

Close-Reading Texts

Inside the Space Station	Exploring Space
Astronauts need to stay healthy on the space station. They work hard while they are up there. Rest is very important. Crew members have private places to sleep. Exercise is important, too. Muscles and bones can grow weak in space. So, astronauts must stay fit. They may use equipment to make sure their bodies stay healthy. Life on the space station sure is interesting!	Mariana didn't want him to go alone. She let go, too. The force of the spinning ring set their speed. They zoomed downward. "We're leaving space," Silas said. "There's the sky." They moved lower and lower toward the ground. Then, they were on the swings again. "Did we just go to space?" Mariana asked. It all felt like a dream, but they knew it wasn't. "I think we did!" Silas answered.

Name: _____ **Date:** _____

Directions: Think about the texts from this unit. Then, respond to the prompt.

Reflect on what you read. What did you find most interesting about space? Did anything you read surprise you? What topic would you like to learn more about in the future?

_____

_____

_____

_____

_____

_____

_____

_____

_____

_____

_____

Name: _____ **Date:** _____

Directions: Write your own Haiku about space. The first line must have 5 syllables. The second line must have 7 syllables. The third line must have 5 syllables again. Then, draw a picture that goes with your poem.

_____

_____

_____

Name: _____ **Date:** _____

Directions: Read the text, and answer the questions.

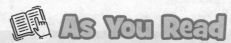
As You Read

Put a ☆ next to information you already knew.

Earthquakes

An earthquake shakes the ground. The earth far below our feet moves. Earthquakes can be a quick jolt. They can be a rolling motion. They can last a second or longer. Earthquakes surprise people when they happen. It is important to stay calm and to get to a safe place.

1. What is this text mostly about?

- Ⓐ shocks
- Ⓑ earthquakes
- Ⓒ rolling motions
- Ⓓ staying calm

2. How long does an earthquake last?

- Ⓐ one second
- Ⓑ many seconds
- Ⓒ it varies
- Ⓓ one minute

3. Which word has the same suffix as *rolling*?

- Ⓐ ball
- Ⓑ rolled
- Ⓒ making
- Ⓓ ring

4. Which words are similar in meaning?

- Ⓐ *calm* and *quick*
- Ⓑ *jolt* and *shake*
- Ⓒ *surprise* and *motion*
- Ⓓ *place* and *safe*

Directions: Read the text, and answer the questions.

Underline information that is new or interesting to you.

Scientists Study Storms

Scientists try to learn from storms. They collect data. They want to be able to predict when a storm is coming. A hurricane is one example. Scientists study wind patterns. They watch how a storm changes. They observe rain levels. They want to give people enough time to get to a safe place.

a map showing weather data

1. What is the main idea?

   (A) Scientists ignore storms.

   (B) Scientists collect data on storms.

   (C) Scientists watch rain levels.

   (D) Scientists learn from storms and warn people.

2. Why do scientists want to predict storms?

   (A) to give people accurate data

   (B) to give people time to get somewhere safe

   (C) to know when to get the best readings

   (D) to know where the storm is headed

3. Which suffix could be added to the root word *come*?

   (A) *–er*

   (B) *–ed*

   (C) *–s*

   (D) *–ion*

4. What does *observe* mean?

   (A) tell people

   (B) watch closely

   (C) move quickly

   (D) live slowly

Directions: Read the text, and answer the questions.

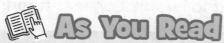 **As You Read**

Put an **!** next to information that surprises you.

Be Prepared

It is important to prepare for disasters. Think about where you live. What happens there? Do you see tornadoes? Are hurricanes common? Is there risk of an earthquake? Prepare for what you may face one day. Better to be safe than sorry!

1. What word describes the main idea?
   - (A) tornadoes
   - (B) risk
   - (C) prepare
   - (D) safe

2. Which suffix does **not** work with the root word *prepare*?
   - (A) –ed
   - (B) –ing
   - (C) –ly
   - (D) –s

3. What is something the text recommends?

   _____

   _____

4. What is another way to say *Better to be safe than sorry*?

   _____

   _____

   _____

Put an **!** next to information that surprises you.

Natural Disasters

A natural disaster is often a sudden event. It is usually intense. It has extreme results. It is caused by natural factors. It might start with rain or heavy winds. A volcano erupts. The Earth shakes. A tsunami hits the coast. These are all natural disasters.

Natural disasters can happen anywhere. They can occur at any time. Some areas are prone to, or likely to have, big storms. Other areas have tornadoes. Tsunamis are a worry for people who live by the ocean. It all depends on where you live.

Disasters can be scary. They can hurt or kill people. They can cause a lot of damage. Buildings can be destroyed. Entire towns can be ruined.

One way to handle disasters is to plan ahead. Planning can keep us safe. It also gives us peace of mind. We know we are ready. Other people help us prepare. Some areas have warnings. They tell people to evacuate to a safe place. They let people know when a big disaster may be on the way. Other disasters happen too quickly. An earthquake can surprise you. There is no warning, but an earthquake kit can help you after the event.

building after a natural disaster

Where do you live? What happens in your town or city? Think ahead. Find out what you need. Make a plan with your family. Be ready! That is the best thing you can do.

135044—180 Days of Reading   © Shell Education

Directions: Read "Natural Disasters." Then, answer the questions.

1. Which gives the best summary of the text?

   A Hurricanes occur only in certain places.

   B Preparing for a tornado takes a lot of time.

   C Preparing for a natural disaster is a smart thing to do.

   D People far from the coast don't need to worry about tsunamis.

2. Which is a strong personal connection to the text?

   A I like to read about tsunamis.

   B Windy days are fun.

   C Waves in a storm are cool.

   D I evacuated once after a hurricane.

3. Which is **not** an example of a natural disaster?

   A tornado

   B hurricane

   C car crash

   D earthquake

4. What does the word *prone* mean?

   A will happen

   B likely to happen

   C won't occur

   D cannot occur

5. Write four important details about natural disasters.

Detail 1	
Detail 2	
Detail 3	
Detail 4	

Name: _____ **Date:** _____

Directions: Reread "Natural Disasters." Then, respond to the prompt.

Answer some questions to reflect on what you read.

- What do you think is most interesting?
- What facts do you think are the most important?
- What else do you want to know about natural disasters?

_____

_____

_____

_____

_____

_____

_____

_____

_____

Name: _____ **Date:** _____

Directions: Read the text, then answer the questions.

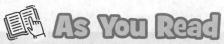 **As You Read**

Think of connections you can make to the text.
Write a ∞ whenever you make connections.

Building the Colony

Once upon a time, there was a queen ant. She was very demanding. But she had good reason. She needed a new home. It had to be big enough for all her babies. The queen commanded her subjects and told them to build rooms. She ordered them to dig tunnels. The worker ants got to work. They built a beautiful colony.

1. Who are the queen's subjects?
   - (A) people of the city
   - (B) worker ants
   - (C) other queens
   - (D) her enemy

2. What do the worker ants build?
   - (A) a city
   - (B) a hive
   - (C) an ant hill
   - (D) a colony

3. What is the singular spelling of *babies*?
   - (A) baby
   - (B) babi
   - (C) babie
   - (D) babe

4. Why is the queen ant so demanding?
   - (A) She is hungry.
   - (B) She needs a new place to live.
   - (C) She doesn't like the worker ants.
   - (D) She is in danger.

Directions: Read the text, and answer the questions.

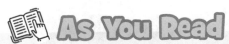 **As You Read**
Circle descriptive words or phrases.

Flood!

Suddenly, the ants felt the ground shake, and saw a flood of water pouring into the colony. The queen ran for her life. The worker ants ran, too. They raced to higher ground. Water swept into the tunnels. It rushed through the rooms. The ants were powerless to stop it. They could only watch.

1. What is the meaning of *powerless*?
   - (A) having power
   - (B) sharing power
   - (C) without power
   - (D) to be strong

2. What makes the ground shake?
   - (A) all the ants running
   - (B) a flood of rushing water
   - (C) a predator chasing them
   - (D) ants in another colony

3. Where do the ants run?
   - (A) up a tree
   - (B) down an empty tunnel
   - (C) to higher ground
   - (D) into a house

4. What is another word for *poured*?
   - (A) dripped
   - (B) gushed
   - (C) sprinkled
   - (D) misted

Name: _____ **Date:** _____

Directions: Read the text, and answer the questions.

 **As You Read**

Underline words or phrases that show or tell how the ants feel.

A Colony Destroyed

Finally, the flooding stopped. The queen ordered the worker ants back to the colony.

"Check it out," she said. "Then come back and report to me."

The worker ants climbed down. They were shocked at what they saw. The tunnels had collapsed. All the rooms were ruined. Everything was soaked with water. It was all destroyed. The ants were very unhappy. They had no idea what to do.

1. What is another word for *unhappy*?

   (A) thrilled

   (B) excited

   (C) confused

   (D) sad

2. Which word is spelled incorrectly?

   (A) flooding

   (B) finally

   (C) soked

   (D) climbed

3. Who does the queen send to check on the colony?

   _____

4. What do you think the ants should do now?

   _____

   _____

   _____

Name: _____   Date: _____

Draw an 👁 next to words that help you visualize the story.

Rebuilding Together

The ants reported back to their queen.

"The colony is destroyed," a worker ant told her. "We are ruined."

But the queen was queen for a reason. She knew how to lead her subjects.

"Nonsense," she said. "We are not ruined. We just have to rebuild!"

The worker ants waited. They expected her to order them to work, and she did. But she surprised them. She did not just watch. She also worked!

Together, the ants formed a line, and each one moved tiny bits of dirt. After a long time, there were empty spaces underground. The ants made rooms and tunnels. A new colony took shape. Naturally, the queen took credit.

"Do you see what we can do when we work together?" she asked.

The worker ants nodded and bowed down to her. They had always known the power of cooperation. And now, they were glad that the queen knew, too.

Directions: Read "Rebuilding Together." Then, answer the questions.

1. What is another word for *surprised*?
   - (A) destroyed
   - (B) ruined
   - (C) shocked
   - (D) thrilled

2. The queen is a good _____.
   - (A) follower
   - (B) leader
   - (C) swimmer
   - (D) speaker

3. What lesson does the queen learn?
   - (A) She learns how to build tunnels.
   - (B) She learns water can destroy tunnels.
   - (C) She learns the importance of cooperation.
   - (D) She learns how to order.

4. What does it mean to rebuild?
   - (A) build less
   - (B) build again
   - (C) build bigger
   - (D) build smaller

5. Compare the characters from the story.

Queen	Ants

Both

Name: _____ **Date:** _____

Directions: Reread "Rebuilding Together." Then, respond to the prompt.

Think of a time you had to rebuild or redo something. How did you feel? How did you overcome it? Explain what happened. Compare your experience to the ants' experiences.

_____

_____

_____

_____

_____

_____

_____

_____

_____

_____

_____

Donation Station

A winter storm is coming! Some people do not have what they need. Now, the community needs your help. Please donate warm coats, blankets, gloves, and scarves here. Spread the word, and let's get prepared together. Thank you!

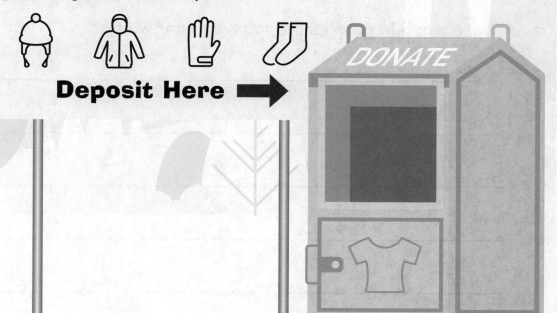

Name: _____ **Date:** _____

Directions: Read "Donation Station." Then, answer the questions.

1. Which warm items are **not** listed?

- (A) blankets
- (B) gloves
- (C) beanies
- (D) scarves

2. What is another word for *donate*?

- (A) receive
- (B) give
- (C) take
- (D) want

3. What is the singular form of *scarves*?

- (A) scarv
- (B) scar
- (C) scarve
- (D) scarf

4. Which word means the opposite of *prepared*?

- (A) ready
- (B) organized
- (C) unprepared
- (D) on time

5. What else might people need to prepare for winter?

_____

_____

_____

_____

_____

DONATIONS

Name: _____ **Date:** _____

Directions: Closely read this text. Then, study the poster on page 203. Look for words with prefixes or suffixes in each text. Write the words in the chart.

Close-Reading Texts

Rebuilding Together
The ants reported back to their queen.
"The colony is destroyed," a worker ant told her. "We are ruined."
But the queen was queen for a reason. She knew how to lead her subjects.
"Nonsense," she said. "We are not ruined. We just have to rebuild!"
The worker ants waited. They expected her to order them to work, and she did. But she surprised them. She did not just watch. She also worked!

Text	Words with a Prefix or Suffix
Rebuilding Together	
Donation Station	

Name: _____ Date: _____

Directions: Closely read these texts. Then, compare the content in the Venn diagram below.

Close-Reading Texts

Natural Disasters	Rebuilding Together
Disasters can be scary. They can hurt or kill people. They can cause a lot of damage. Buildings can be destroyed. Entire towns can be ruined.	The worker ants climbed down. They were shocked at what they saw. The tunnels had collapsed. All the rooms were ruined. Everything was soaked with water. It was all destroyed. The ants were very unhappy. They had no idea what to do.

Natural Disasters

Both

Rebuilding Together

Name: _____ **Date:** _____

Directions: Think about the texts from this unit. Then, respond to the prompt.

What do these three texts have in common? What is the central theme or lesson? Give examples from the texts when writing.

_____

_____

_____

_____

_____

_____

_____

_____

_____

_____

_____

_____

Name: _____ **Date:** _____

Directions: Think about a way to help your local community. Design a poster to advertise this idea. Include who, what, when, and where this event or activity takes place.

135044—180 Days of Reading   © Shell Education

Name: _____ **Date:** _____

Directions: Read the text, and answer the questions.

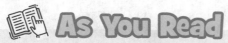 As You Read

Put a ☆ next to information you already knew.

Love of Baseball

Many people enjoy baseball. They like to play and watch it. It is a popular sport. A lot of people like Major League Baseball. Players get paid to play in these games. There are a lot of teams. The Chicago Cubs is one team. They have played since 1876. They are the oldest team to stay in the same city.

1. What is special about the Chicago Cubs?
   - (A) They are part of the major league.
   - (B) People enjoy watching them.
   - (C) They are the oldest team to stay in the same city.
   - (D) They win a lot of games.

2. When were the Chicago Cubs formed?
   - (A) 1877
   - (B) 1786
   - (C) 1867
   - (D) 1876

3. What is the root word in *oldest*?
   - (A) old
   - (B) est
   - (C) dest
   - (D) st

4. Based on the text, what does *league* mean?
   - (A) a group of sports teams that play against each other
   - (B) a team that has played for a long time
   - (C) a team in Chicago
   - (D) a bunch of teams from different sports

Directions: Read the text, and answer the questions.

Underline information that is new or interesting to you.

Equality for All

People are not always treated the same. This unequal treatment is called *discrimination*. In the past, men had more rights than women. Women could not vote. They could not own houses or have jobs. This has changed, but it took many years for change to come. Laws have been passed to make sure it stays this way. Today, women in most places have the same rights as men.

people voting

1. What is the main idea?
   - Ⓐ Women can now vote.
   - Ⓑ Discrimination against women has changed.
   - Ⓒ Women have the same rights as long ago.
   - Ⓓ Women and men do not have the same rights.

2. Why is discrimination no longer allowed?
   - Ⓐ It happened to men.
   - Ⓑ It is hard to find a job for everyone.
   - Ⓒ It is against the law now.
   - Ⓓ Women today still can't do what men can.

3. What is the suffix in the word *changed*?
   - Ⓐ *–ed*
   - Ⓑ *–ged*
   - Ⓒ *–d*
   - Ⓓ *ch–*

4. Which word means to treat unfairly?
   - Ⓐ changed
   - Ⓑ women
   - Ⓒ people
   - Ⓓ discrimination

Name: _____ **Date:** _____

Directions: Read the text, and answer the questions.

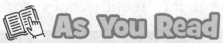 **As You Read**

Put an **!** next to information that surprises you.

Rosa Parks

Rosa Parks stood up for herself. Rosa Parks was a Black woman. One day in 1955, she refused to follow the law. She was riding on a bus, and she had to give up her seat to a white person. This was the law. But she did not give up her seat. So, she was arrested. Her actions changed the world. She helped spark the civil rights movement.

1. In what year did Rosa Parks refuse to follow the law?

- Ⓐ 1954
- Ⓑ 1955
- Ⓒ 1956
- Ⓓ 1957

2. Why did Rosa Parks refuse to give up her seat?

- Ⓐ She thought the law was unfair.
- Ⓑ She didn't like the other person who wanted her seat.
- Ⓒ Her seat was the best seat on the bus.
- Ⓓ She was stubborn.

3. What movement started because of Rosa Park's actions?

_____

4. How do you think Rosa Parks felt after she was arrested?

_____

_____

Name: _____ **Date:** _____

 **As You Read**

Put an **!** next to information that surprises you.

An Inspirational Man

Jackie Robinson was a baseball player. He was very famous. He was born in 1919. He was a Black man. His life was hard. He faced discrimination. People were not always nice to him. Sometimes, they treated him badly.

As a child, Robinson loved sports. He was a good athlete. He was strong and fast. After going to college, he joined the army. Then, he made a choice. He wanted to play baseball. This was in 1944.

At the time, baseball teams were separate. White players had their own teams. Black players had their own, too. Robinson was chosen for a team. It was a team of only white players. It was a hard time for him. Some people wanted him to stop playing. They wanted him on another team. Some of his teammates agreed. Other teams did not want to play against him.

But not all people felt like this. Some people stood up for him. His manager was loyal to him. This helped other people treat Robinson better. People began to change their minds. All the while, Robinson showed that he could play ball. He was an amazing athlete. He changed people's minds. That was a victory!

Directions: Read "An Inspirational Man." Then, answer the questions.

1. Which shows a strong connection to the text?
   - (A) I need to learn to play baseball.
   - (B) I am angry when people do not include me.
   - (C) I work through hard times and don't give up.
   - (D) When life is tough, it's time to take a break.

2. How does the author describe Robinson's life?
   - (A) It was easy.
   - (B) It was scary.
   - (C) It was nice.
   - (D) It was difficult.

3. What does *loyal* mean?
   - (A) upset with someone
   - (B) expressing support and dedication for someone
   - (C) playing nicely with someone
   - (D) ignoring someone

4. Robinson had a difficult life because _____.
   - (A) baseball is a hard sport
   - (B) people discriminated against him
   - (C) he did not like to play baseball
   - (D) he was well-known

5. Write four major events in Jackie Robinson's life. Write them in the order they occurred.

Event 1	Jackie Robinson was born in 1919.
Event 2	
Event 3	
Event 4	

Name: _____ **Date:** _____

Directions: Reread "An Inspirational Man." Then, respond to the prompt.

Imagine Jackie Robinson is still alive. Write him a letter. Tell him what you think about his life. Ask him some questions.

_____

_____,

_____

_____

_____

_____

_____

_____

_____

_____

_____,

_____

Directions: Read the text, then answer the questions.

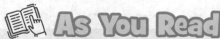 **As You Read**

Think of connections you can make to the text.
Write a ∞ whenever you make connections.

A Big Dream

Lisa loved playing baseball. She played all the time with her friends. She watched a lot of games in her free time. She always wore a baseball hat. She kept a glove nearby at all times. She even read a book about Jackie Robinson. He was a famous baseball player. She had a big dream. She wanted to be a professional baseball player.

1. What sport does Lisa love?
   - (A) basketball
   - (B) baseball
   - (C) soccer
   - (D) tennis

2. Who does Lisa play with?
   - (A) her parents
   - (B) her sister
   - (C) her friends
   - (D) her brother

3. What does Lisa always keep nearby?
   - (A) a ball
   - (B) a glove
   - (C) a book
   - (D) a jersey

4. Which word has three syllables?
   - (A) baseball
   - (B) dreamed
   - (C) famous
   - (D) Robinson

Name: _____   Date: _____

Directions: Read the text, and answer the questions.

 **As You Read**

Underline words or phrases that describe the main character.

Worst Player Ever?

Lisa tried hard when she played baseball in P.E. class, but she was always picked last for teams. That made her feel bad about herself. She missed balls she meant to catch, and she often struck out when she was up to bat. Some of the kids in her class laughed at her. They thought she wasn't a very good player. Lisa wasn't sure what to think, but she worried about it a lot. Maybe they were right.

1. Which verb is in the past tense?
   - (A) played
   - (B) feel
   - (C) worry
   - (D) make

2. What is the base word in *tries*?
   - (A) tri
   - (B) try
   - (C) tried
   - (D) trying

3. Why does Lisa feel badly about herself?
   - (A) She is shy.
   - (B) She is smart.
   - (C) She is picked last for baseball.
   - (D) She is energetic.

4. Why do some kids laugh at Lisa?
   - (A) She strikes out.
   - (B) She runs too fast.
   - (C) She loves baseball.
   - (D) She tries hard.

Name: _____ **Date:** _____

Directions: Read the text, and answer the questions.

 **As You Read**

Draw an 👁 next to words that help you visualize the story.

Solo Practice Session

If I'm not a good player, I have to get better, Lisa told herself. So, she put on her baseball hat and grabbed her glove. She went outside to practice.

Lisa threw the ball. But she soon realized she couldn't practice catching alone. She realized she couldn't practice hitting, either. She had nobody to throw the ball to her. She knew she should ask a friend for help, but she felt embarrassed. Who would want to help her now? Even a friend might laugh.

---

1. What does Lisa do right after she put on her baseball hat?

   - (A) She grabs her hat.
   - (B) She grabs her glove.
   - (C) She practices.
   - (D) She laughs.

2. Which word has two syllables?

   - (A) better
   - (B) good
   - (C) catch
   - (D) throw

3. Why does Lisa feel embarrassed?

   _____

   _____

4. What would you do if you were in Lisa's situation?

   _____

   _____

 **As You Read**

Draw a ♡ next to your favorite part(s) of the story.

A Magical Moment

The next day at school, Lisa's P.E. teacher announced a surprise.

"It's just for a few lucky players," he said. Lisa looked down at the ground. She knew she wouldn't be picked. "Lucky players" had to mean the best. But then her teacher called her name.

"Lisa," he said. "You can be first to meet our guest coach. He's outside waiting for you."

Lisa was shocked, but she quickly went to the backfield. When she saw the coach, she gasped. "You're Jackie Robinson!" she exclaimed. "How is this possible?"

Jackie laughed. "Never mind that, kid," he said. "I'm here to work on your game. Let's go!"

Jackie worked with Lisa. He helped her get better at catching, throwing, and hitting. Lisa was happy to have his help. But when they were done, Jackie noticed she still looked sad.

"What's wrong?" he asked.

"Nobody believes I'm a good player," Lisa said. "I'll probably still get picked last for teams. I'll never be a professional."

"Not with an attitude like that you won't," Jackie agreed. "You have to believe in yourself."

Lisa was about to argue. But then she remembered what she'd learned about Jackie. He had to struggle to become a professional baseball player, too.

Just then, Lisa woke up. She was in her bed. It was just a dream! But it felt so real. And her arm was even sore. She thought of what she learned from Jackie in the dream. Then, she thought of her real dream to be great at baseball.

I'll try, she thought to herself. Then she corrected herself. *I'll never give up.*

Directions: Read "A Magical Moment." Then, answer the questions.

1. What skill does Jackie Robinson **not** help Lisa with?

   Ⓐ catching

   Ⓑ running

   Ⓒ throwing

   Ⓓ hitting

2. Why is Lisa still sad after she gets help?

   Ⓐ She is very tired.

   Ⓑ She doesn't care for Jackie Robinson.

   Ⓒ She doesn't think anyone believes in her.

   Ⓓ She is not feeling well.

3. Why does Lisa gasp when she sees Jackie Robinson?

   Ⓐ She is shocked.

   Ⓑ She is sad.

   Ⓒ She is embarrassed.

   Ⓓ She is hurt.

4. What is another meaning for *picked* in this text?

   Ⓐ pulled

   Ⓑ chosen

   Ⓒ lost

   Ⓓ poked

5. Describe the beginning, middle, and end of the story.

Beginning	Middle	End

Name: _____ **Date:** _____

Directions: Reread "A Magical Moment." Then, respond to the prompt.

Think of a time you didn't give up. Write about what
happened and how it felt to not give up. How was this similar
to Lisa's experience? How was it different?

_____

_____

_____

_____

_____

_____

_____

_____

_____

_____

_____

Name: _____ Date: _____

Ballpark Sign

Ballpark Rules

No outside food or drinks.

No pets allowed in the park.

Shoes and shirt must be worn at all times.

No cowbells, airhorns, or other noisemakers.

Do not climb fences.

Thank you for your cooperation!

Name: _____ **Date:** _____

Directions: Read "Ballpark Rules." Then, answer the questions.

1. Which word means the same as *cooperation*?
   - Ⓐ disagreement
   - Ⓑ helping
   - Ⓒ silliness
   - Ⓓ selfish

2. Which word has two syllables?
   - Ⓐ food
   - Ⓑ airhorns
   - Ⓒ drinks
   - Ⓓ park

3. What must be worn in the ballpark at all times?
   - Ⓐ hat and shoes
   - Ⓑ shirt and shorts
   - Ⓒ shoes and shirt
   - Ⓓ shirt and gloves

4. Which of the following is not allowed in the park?
   - Ⓐ hat
   - Ⓑ red shirt
   - Ⓒ shoes
   - Ⓓ outside food

5. Why do you think noisemakers are not allowed in the ballpark?

   _____

   _____

   _____

   _____

   _____

Directions: Closely read these texts. Then, study the rules sign on page 221. Look for words about baseball in the texts. Write the words in the chart.

Close-Reading Texts

An Inspirational Man	A Magical Moment
Jackie Robinson was a baseball player. He was very famous. He was born in 1919. He was a Black man. His life was hard. He faced discrimination. People were not always nice to him. Sometimes, they treated him badly. As a child, Robinson loved sports. He was a good athlete. He was strong and fast.	Jackie laughed. "Never mind that, kid," he said. "I'm here to work on your game. Let's go!" Jackie worked with Lisa. He helped her get better at catching, throwing, and hitting. Lisa was happy to have his help. But when they were done, Jackie noticed she still looked sad. "What's wrong?" he asked. "Nobody believes I'm a good player," Lisa said. "I'll probably still get picked last for teams. I'll never be a professional."

Text	Baseball Words
An Inspirational Man	
A Magical Moment	
Ballpark Rules	

Name: _____ Date: _____

Directions: Closely read these texts. Then, write the authors' purpose for each of these texts.

Close-Reading Texts

An Inspirational Man	A Magical Moment
But not all people felt like this. Some people stood up for him. His manager was loyal to him. This helped other people treat Robinson better. People began to change their minds. All the while, Robinson showed that he could play ball. He was an amazing athlete. He changed people's minds. That was a victory!	Just then, Lisa woke up. She was in her bed. It was just a dream! But it felt so real. And her arm was even sore. She thought of what she learned from Jackie in the dream. Then, she thought of her real dream to be great at baseball. *I'll try*, she thought to herself. Then she corrected herself. *I'll never give up.*

Authors' Purpose

Why did the author write the text? What do they want readers to know or learn? How do they want readers to feel?

An Inspirational Man	A Magical Moment
_____	_____
_____	_____
_____	_____
_____	_____
_____	_____

135044—180 Days of Reading

Name: _____ **Date:** _____

Directions: Think about the texts from this unit. Then, respond to the prompt.

> Think of someone famous that you look up to. What would it be like to meet them? What would you want to say to them? Draw a picture of you meeting this person.

_____

_____

_____

_____

_____

_____

_____

_____

_____

_____

_____

Name: _____ **Date:** _____

Directions: Think of a place other than a ballpark that might have rules. It can be real or make-believe. Write a list of rules for this place.

Rules for _____

_____

_____

_____

_____

_____

_____

_____

_____

_____

_____

_____

Standards Correlations

Shell Education is committed to producing educational materials that are research and standards based. To support this effort, this resource is correlated to the academic standards of all 50 states, the District of Columbia, the Department of Defense Dependent Schools, and the Canadian provinces. A correlation is also provided for key professional educational organizations.

To print a customized correlation report for your state, visit our website at **www.tcmpub.com/administrators/correlations** and follow the online directions. If you require assistance in printing correlation reports, please contact the Customer Service Department at 1-800-858-7339.

Standards Overview

The Every Student Succeeds Act (ESSA) mandates that all states adopt challenging academic standards that help students meet the goal of college and career readiness. While many states already adopted academic standards prior to ESSA, the act continues to hold states accountable for detailed and comprehensive standards. Standards are designed to focus instruction and guide adoption of curricula. They define the knowledge, skills, and content students should acquire at each level. Standards are also used to develop standardized tests to evaluate students' academic progress. State standards are used in the development of our resources, so educators can be assured they meet state academic requirements.

College and Career Readiness

Today's college and career readiness (CCR) standards offer guidelines for preparing K–12 students with the knowledge and skills that are necessary to succeed in postsecondary job training and education. CCR standards include the Common Core State Standards as well as other state-adopted standards such as the Texas Essential Knowledge and Skills. The standards found on page 228 describe the content presented throughout the lessons.

TESOL and WIDA Standards

English language development standards are integrated within each lesson to enable English learners to work toward proficiency in English while learning content—developing the skills and confidence in listening, speaking, reading, and writing. The standards found in the digital resources describe the language objectives presented throughout the lessons.

Standards Correlations (cont.)

180 Days of Reading for Second Grade, 2nd Edition offers a full page of daily reading comprehension and word analysis practice activities for each day of the school year.

Every second-grade unit provides questions and activities tied to a wide variety of language arts standards, providing students the opportunity for regular practice in reading comprehension, word recognition, and writing. The focus of the first two weeks in each unit alternates between nonfiction and fiction standards, with the third week focusing on both, as students read nontraditional texts and complete paired-text activities.

Reading Comprehension

Read and comprehend complex literary and informational texts independently and proficiently.

Read closely to determine what the text says explicitly. Ask and answer questions about the text and make logical inferences.

Determine central ideas or themes of a text and analyze their development; summarize the key supporting details and ideas.

Analyze how and why individuals, events, or ideas develop and interact over the course of a text.

Recognize and analyze genre-specific characteristics, structures, and purposes within and across diverse texts.

Use metacognitive skills to both develop and deepen comprehension of texts.

Analyze how two or more texts address similar themes or topics in order to build knowledge or to compare the approaches the authors take.

Assess how point of view or purpose shapes the content and style of texts.

Reading Foundational Skills

Know and apply grade-level phonics and word analysis skills in decoding words.

Language and Vocabulary Acquisition

Determine or clarify the meaning of unknown and multiple-meaning words and phrases by using context clues, analyzing meaningful word parts, and consulting general and specialized reference materials, as appropriate.

Demonstrate understanding of figurative language, word relationships, and nuances in word meanings.

Writing

Produce clear and coherent writing in which the development, organization, and style are appropriate to task, purpose, genre, and audience.

Respond to and draw evidence from literary or informational texts to show analysis, reflection, and research.

Writing Rubric

Score students' written response using the rubric below. Display the rubric for students to reference as they write. A student version of this rubric is provided in the digital resources.

Points	Criteria
4	• Uses an appropriate organizational sequence to produce very clear and coherent writing. • Uses descriptive language that develops or clarifies ideas. • Engages the reader. • Uses a style very appropriate to task, purpose, and audience.
3	• Uses an organizational sequence to produce clear and coherent writing. • Uses descriptive language that develops or clarifies ideas. • Engages the reader. • Uses a style appropriate to task, purpose, and audience.
2	• Uses an organizational sequence to produce somewhat clear and coherent writing. • Uses some descriptive language that develops or clarifies ideas. • Engages the reader in some way. • Uses a style somewhat appropriate to task, purpose, and audience.
1	• Does not use an organized sequence; the writing is not clear or coherent. • Uses little descriptive language to develop or clarify ideas. • Does not engage the reader. • Does not use a style appropriate to task, purpose, or audience.
0	• Offers no writing or does not respond to the assignment presented.

References Cited

Gough, Philip B., and William E. Tunmer. 1986. "Decoding, Reading, and Reading Disability." *Remedial and Special Education* 7 (1): 6-10.

Marzano, Robert. 2010. "When Practice Makes Perfect...Sense." *Educational Leadership* 68 (3): 81–83.

National Reading Panel. 2000. *Report of the National Reading Panel: Teaching Children to Read. Report of the Subgroups*. Washington, D.C.: U.S. Department of Health and Human Services, National Institutes of Health.

Scarborough, Hollis S. 2001. "Connecting Early Language and Literacy to Later Reading (Dis)abilities: Evidence, Theory, and Practice." In *Handbook of Early Literacy Research*, edited by Susan B. Neuman and David K. Dickinson, 97-110. New York: Guilford.

Soalt, Jennifer. 2005. "Bringing Together Fictional and Informational Texts to Improve Comprehension." *The Reading Teacher* 58 (7): 680–683.

Answer Key

Unit 1

Week 1

Day 1 (page 11)
1. D 3. C
2. C 4. A

Day 2 (page 12)
1. B 3. B
2. D 4. C

Day 3 (page 13)
1. C 2. B
3. The main idea of the text is shark attacks in the ocean.
4. Sharks sometimes mistake humans for food.

Day 4 (page 15)
1. C 3. C
2. B 4. A
5. Drawings should include very little water in the low tide picture and lots of water in the high tide picture. Low tide should include some sea creatures.

Day 5 (page 16)
Drawings and sentences should likely include sea stars, fish, seashells, crabs, seaweed, etc.

Week 2

Day 1 (page 17)
1. B 3. A
2. D 4. B

Day 2 (page 18)
1. C 3. A
2. B 4. B

Day 3 (page 19)
1. B 2. D
3. He is too hungry to swim. He wants to eat first.
4. Answers should describe how students would feel if a seagull ate their sandwich.

Day 4 (page 21)
1. B 3. C
2. A 4. B
5. Answers should include nouns and verbs, such as sandwich, sandcastle, waves, jump, finish, and dropped.

Day 5 (page 22)
Answers should include new endings to the story.

Week 3

Day 1 (page 24)
1. B 3. C
2. A 4. B
5. Answers should include ideas about what else could be added to the flyer.

Day 2 (page 25)
Example

Text	Ocean/Beach Words
Investigating Tide Pools	tide pool, beach, water, high tide, low tide, ocean
A Game with the Gulls	waves, sandcastle, sand
Seagull Flyer	beach, seagulls, sand, water, sea, sun, fish, ocean

Day 3 (page 26)
Author's purpose for "Investigating Tide Pools" is to teach/provide information about tide pools.

Author's purpose for "A Game with the Gulls" is entertainment.

Day 4 (page 27)
Responses should include what students will bring to the beach, who is going, and what events will happen there.

Day 5 (page 28)
Information on flyers should detail what people should and should not do while at the beach.

Unit 2

Week 1

Day 1 (page 29)
1. B 3. B
2. D 4. D

Day 2 (page 30)
1. C 3. B
2. B 4. D

Day 3 (page 31)
1. B 2. C
3. The main idea is that plants can go extinct.
4. People should worry because we need plants to survive.

Day 4 (page 33)
1. A 3. D
2. B 4. B
5. Facts should include newly learned information about ecosystems.

Answer Key *(cont.)*

Day 5 (page 34)

Answers should include reflections on how the connectedness of ecosystems reminds students of their lives and a corresponding picture.

Week 2

Day 1 (page 35)

1. B
2. A
3. C
4. D

Day 2 (page 36)

1. A
2. D
3. B
4. B

Day 3 (page 37)

1. C
2. A

3. Possible answers include finding ways to save/help endangered plants and animals.

4. Possible answers include asking adults, checking the internet, reading books, and visiting zoos and nurseries.

Day 4 (page 39)

1. B
2. C
3. B
4. C

5. Beginning—Class discussion about what they'll see on their walk.
Middle—The class goes on a walk and she thinks about all the endangered species she learned about.
End—Her teacher calls her a superhero for helping endangered species.

Day 5 (page 40)

Answers should describe walks and what plants and animals students hope to see and include a corresponding picture.

Week 3

Day 1 (page 42)

1. B
2. C
3. A
4. A

5. Sandcastles can get in the way when turtles need to nest.

Day 2 (page 43)

Text	Action Verbs
Ecosystems	depend, need, survive, die, changes, imagine, hunted, wanted, fished, fishing
My Secret Is Out	taking, raise, guesses, see, bet, ask, answers
Sea Turtle Poster	save, building, knock, nest

Day 3 (page 44)

Author's purpose for writing, "Ecosystems," is to educate readers about endangered species.

Author's purpose for writing, "My Secret Is Out," is to entertain readers while also teaching about endangered species.

Day 4 (page 45)

Answers should detail superpowers and how students will use them to solve problems and include a corresponding picture.

Day 5 (page 46)

Posters should show and detail fictional endangered plants or animals.

Unit 3

Week 1

Day 1 (page 47)

1. B
2. C
3. D
4. C

Day 2 (page 48)

1. B
2. A
3. D
4. B

Day 3 (page 49)

1. D
2. A

3. Answers should include what pet students would want.

4. Examples: birds, fish, or any other reptile/amphibian

Day 4 (page 51)

1. C
2. A
3. A
4. B

5.

Cats	Dogs
Mostly indoor pets	Need outside space
Like high places	Like dog parks
	Like to go on walks
Both	
Like to play	
Make great pets	

Day 5 (page 52)

Answers should discuss pets students would want, describe their needs, and tell how to provide a happy and healthy life for them and include a picture.

Week 2

Day 1 (page 53)

1. B
2. C
3. A
4. D

Day 2 (page 54)

1. B
2. D
3. A
4. C

Answer Key *(cont.)*

Day 3 (page 55)

1. A   2. C

3. The parakeet is confused because he's not sure if he has a friend or if it's his reflection in the mirror.

4. Answers should explain connections to the text.

Day 4 (page 57)

1. B   3. C
2. A   4. B

5. Characters: Violet the parakeet and the family (father, daughter, child); Setting: back home, dancing, phone call

Day 5 (page 58)

Answers should include how the prank would be different.

Week 3

Day 1 (page 60)

1. A   3. D
2. B   4. C

5. Possible answers: pay rate, hours

Day 2 (page 61)

Examples

Text	Nouns
The Right Pet for Your Home	pet, farm, apartment, animal, room, area
My Funny Phone Prank	family, home, people, hands, claws, fingers, music, toys, ball, surprise, treat
Dog Walker Ad	dog, park, job, day

Day 3 (page 62)

Author's purpose for "The Right Pet for Your Home" is education.

Author's purpose for "My Funny Phone Prank" is entertainment.

Day 4 (page 63)

Answers should include questions for the dog owner and why the job is desired.

Day 5 (page 64)

Advertisements should explain help that is needed with a pet.

Unit 4

Week 1

Day 1 (page 65)

1. A   3. B
2. C   4. D

Day 2 (page 66)

1. B   3. C
2. B   4. A

Day 3 (page 67)

1. C   2. C

3. The main idea is that there are millions of stars to see in the night sky.

4. Answers should include whether students think the night sky is beautiful and why or why not.

Day 4 (page 69)

1. C   3. D
2. B   4. C

5. Main idea: Nocturnal animals are awake at night. Details will vary about owls and cats and their habits.

Day 5 (page 70)

Answers should describe what a chosen nocturnal animal does at night and include a picture.

Week 2

Day 1 (page 71)

1. B   3. A
2. C   4. C

Day 2 (page 72)

1. B   3. C
2. B   4. C

Day 3 (page 73)

1. C   2. A

3. Possible answers: rest, sleep, eat something healthy, stretch, exercise, etc.

4. He is very tired from the heavy basket and is surprised how long the trip is taking.

Day 4 (page 75)

1. B   3. C
2. A   4. A

5. Problem: Darkness is let out of the basket.
Solution: Bat collects the darkness all night long and once it seeps out he does it all over again, every night.

Day 5 (page 76)

Answers should include a story of what would happen if Fox and Owl never opened the basket and should have an ending about how darkness was created.

Week 3

Day 1 (page 78)

1. B   3. D
2. C   4. B

5. Diurnal means to be active in the day and at night.

Answer Key (cont.)

Day 2 (page 79)

Text	Two-Syllable Words
What Comes Alive at Night	middle, people, other, alive, creatures, alert, awake, during, survive
How Night Came to Be: Part 4	spotted, basket, wondered, inside, over, open, answered, resist
Animal Poster	many, people, active, worry, about, distance

Day 3 (page 80)

Author's purpose for "What Comes Alive at Night" is to educate readers.

Author's purpose for "How Night Came to Be" is entertainment.

Day 4 (page 81)

Answers should include when a student touched or played something they weren't supposed to and what happened. Answers should compare their story to the text.

Day 5 (page 82)

Posters should include a picture of a new nocturnal animal, a name, and a list of special characteristics.

Unit 5

Week 1

Day 1 (page 83)
1. C
3. A
2. B
4. B

Day 2 (page 84)
1. B
3. C
2. B
4. D

Day 3 (page 85)
1. B
2. A
3. The main idea is that a globe is a model of Earth, which is always changing.
4. Possible answers should include reasons globes have different colors, such as to show different countries or landforms.

Day 4 (page 87)
1. A
3. C
2. D
4. B
5. Main idea: Maps show us different types of information.
Details: Possible answers should include symbols, key, legend, compass rose, and scale.

Day 5 (page 88)
Answers should either tell of a time when a student used a map and how it helped or when they needed a map and how it would have helped.

Week 2

Day 1 (page 89)
1. A
3. C
2. C
4. B

Day 2 (page 90)
1. C
3. B
2. A
4. C

Day 3 (page 91)
1. B
2. C
3. The narrator uses garden tools to bury the loot.
4. The narrator makes a map.

Day 4 (page 93)
1. B
3. C
2. B
4. C
5. Check answers for the correct events in order.

Day 5 (page 94)
Answers should include connections and specific details students made with the text.

Week 3

Day 1 (page 96)
1. B
3. C
2. D
4. B
5. Possible answers should include a few more ways to be a kind pirate.

Day 2 (page 97)

Text	Nouns
Parts of a Map	maps, picture, place, roads, river, weather, objects, symbols, line
A Real Treasure Map	treasure map, treasure, pirates, swords, landmarks, backyard, house, swing set, arrows
Kind Pirate List	pirate, people, plank, treasure, map

Day 3 (page 98)

Author's purpose for "Parts of a Map" is education.

Author's purpose for "A Real Treasure Map" is entertainment.

Day 4 (page 99)

Content of letters should be in friendly letter format from the point of view of one pirate to another.

Day 5 (page 100)

Maps must include keys and be drawn to scale. The steps for making a map might include: make a scale, mark important places with symbols, create a key.

Unit 6

Week 1

Day 1 (page 101)
1. C 3. A
2. D 4. B

Day 2 (page 102)
1. C 3. B
2. B 4. C

Day 3 (page 103)
1. B 2. A
3. Most cars run on gas.
4. Exhaust is used gas that pollutes the air.

Day 4 (page 105)
1. C 3. B
2. D 4. C
5. Possible facts: famous man, started a company, made cars, changed the way people lived, contributed to racing cars/NASCAR

Day 5 (page 106)
1. Answers should describe what it is like to drive a race car and include a picture.

Week 2

Day 1 (page 107)
1. C 3. C
2. B 4. B

Day 2 (page 108)
1. C 3. D
2. B 4. A

Day 3 (page 109)
1. C 2. B
3. Johnny's favorite animal is a tiger.
4. Answers should include details of how students would decorate their own toy cars.

Day 4 (page 111)
1. B 3. D
2. C 4. C
5. Beginning: Johnny and his father bring his car to school. Middle: They all race their cars. End: Tyo wins the race and Johnny wins best animal car.

Day 5 (page 112)

Answers should include whether students like the end of the story. If they don't, they should write a new ending and explain why they changed it.

Week 3

Day 1 (page 114)
1. C 3. B
2. C 4. B
5. Possible answers: height requirement, wheel size, color restrictions, etc.

Day 2 (page 115)

Text	Nouns
The Racetrack	famous, made, making, today
The Race	Saturday, race
Brochure	weight

Day 3 (page 116)

Answers will vary, but the scene from "The Racetrack" will likely include the oval track with a race car and the scene from "Race Day" will likely include the boys with their cards and/or their trophies.

Day 4 (page 117)

Content of letters must follow friendly letter format.

Day 5 (page 118)

Answers should include directions for something students know how to do or make, with a list of steps and a corresponding picture.

Unit 7

Week 1

Day 1 (page 119)
1. B 3. B
2. D 4. C

Day 2 (page 120)
1. A 3. D
2. B 4. C

Answer Key (cont.)

Day 3 (page 121)
1. B 2. C
3. The first robot bug looked like a dragonfly.
4. They move by vibrating or flying.

Day 4 (page 123)
1. D 3. B
2. C 4. A
5. Event 1: The first rover landed in 1997.
Event 2: In 2003, two more rovers arrived.
Event 3: In 2012, a fourth rover arrived.
Event 4: In 2021, a fifth rover landed on Mars.

Day 5 (page 124)
Answers should include what it would be like to go to Mars, how they might use a Mars Rover, and include a corresponding picture.

Week 2

Day 1 (page 125)
1. C 3. C
2. A 4. D

Day 2 (page 126)
1. B 3. D
2. B 4. D

Day 3 (page 127)
1. A 2. C
3. It is fiction because an android is looking through a telescope and able to think.
4. Answers should include types of food.

Day 4 (page 129)
1. A 3. B
2. D 4. B
5. Problem: The robots are not alone; there is an army of creatures ready for battle.
Solution: The robots are badly defeated and they leave.

Day 5 (page 130)
Answers should include a new ending to the story with a corresponding picture.

Week 3

Day 1 (page 132)
1. B 3. B
2. C 4. A
5. The author wants the owner to describe it first, making sure it's really their dog.

Day 2 (page 133)

Text	Two-Syllable Words
The Mars Rovers	believe, robots, rovers, around, pictures, carry, study, weather, about, planet
Into the Future	robots, command, center, ready, something, alone, other, army, creatures
Found in Central Park	Central, fountain, robot, someone, describe, belongs

Day 3 (page 134)
Author's purpose for "The Mars Rovers" is to educate readers.

Author's purpose for "Into the Future" is to entertain readers.

Day 4 (page 135)
Answers should include details about a new robot invention, what it will do, what problem it will solve, and a corresponding picture.

Day 5 (page136)
Robot inventions and posters will vary.

Unit 8

Week 1

Day 1 (page 137)
1. C 3. B
2. A 4. B

Day 2 (page 138)
1. B 3. C
2. A 4. D

Day 3 (page 139)
1. D
2. B
3. It is unique because it is both a continent and a country.
4. One might look on a map or do research on the computer.

Day 4 (page 141)
1. B 3. B
2. C 4. D
5. Main idea: France is a diverse country in Europe that many people like to visit.
Details: Answers may reference France's age, its landscape, its food, or its tourism industry.

Day 5 (page 142)
Answers should include details about what students find interesting about France and why, and a corresponding picture.

Answer Key (cont.)

Week 2

Day 1 (page 143)

1.	C	3.	A
2.	B	4.	B

Day 2 (page 144)

1.	C	3.	C
2.	A	4.	B

Day 3 (page 145)

1.	B	2.	C

3. They are getting information online.
4. Answers should include what students would like to learn about France.

Day 4 (page 147)

1.	B	3.	C
2.	B	4.	D

5. baguette, brie, crepes, macarons

Day 5 (page 148)

Stories might include these details: try more French foods, find parks or things for kids to do in France, visit the Eiffel Tower, or make some French art.

Week 3

Day 1 (page 150)

1.	D	3.	B
2.	C	4.	A

5. Answers should include which dessert from the text students would most like to order and why it would be the best.

Day 2 (page 151)

Text	Nouns
France	France, country, Europe, capital, Paris, part, world, nations, humans, years, landscape, beaches, Mediterranean Sea
A Delicious Vacation	sights, France, movie, restaurant, family, kitchen, food
Les Desserts	Tarte Tatin, apple, pastry, Crème Caramel, caramel, custard, Éclair, Dame Blanche, ice cream, sauce

Day 3 (page 152)

France: visitors, beaches, mountains, Paris

Both: French, eat

A Delicious Vacation: family, dialogue, dessert

Day 4 (page 153)

Letter content should follow friendly letter format.

Day 5 (page 154)

Menus should include an appetizer, main dish, dessert, pricing, brief descriptions, and a picture of one menu item.

Unit 9

Week 1

Day 1 (page 155)

1.	B	3.	D
2.	C	4.	B

Day 2 (page 156)

1.	D	3.	A
2.	B	4.	D

Day 3 (page 157)

1.	A	2.	C

3. Answers should include a question students would ask the Magic 8 Ball.
4. Answers should choose a toy (e.g., Legos, Play-Doh, or Magic 8 Ball) and explain why the student chose it.

Day 4 (page 159)

1.	B	3.	C
2.	C	4.	D

5. Uses for Silly Putty: play with it as a toy, copy comic book pictures, use it to pick up dirt, squeeze it to train muscles, hold tools in place in space

Day 5 (page 160)

Answers should include what students would use Silly Putty for and a corresponding picture.

Week 2

Day 1 (page 161)

1.	B	3.	B
2.	A	4.	C

Day 2 (page 162)

1.	C	3.	B
2.	B	4.	A

Day 3 (page 163)

1.	C	2.	B

3. Everyone looked at each other because nobody knew the new rules.
4. Answers should describe a feeling.

Answer Key (cont.)

Day 4 (page 165)
1. B 3. A
2. C 4. B
5. Problem: Nobody agreed/liked the rules for the game they made up.
Solution: They will meet again tomorrow to make new rules they all like.

Day 5 (page 166)
Answers should include what game rule students might change and what rule they would add.

Week 3

Day 1 (page 168)
1. B 3. D
2. B 4. A
5. Answers should include one step students would change or add to the instructions for the game.

Day 2 (page 169)

Text	Two-Syllable Words
An Accidental Invention	silly, putty, plastic, squishy, stretchy, trying, rubber
Making Rules for a Made-Up Game	Jazmine, pretend, talking, parrot, Polly, cracker, middle, Ari, Elise, around, kicking, soccer, Colton, sidelines, Katy, open
How to Play	TV, player, players, scatter, closes, other, becomes, avoid, being, calling, squatting

Day 3 (page 170)
Author's purpose for "An Accidental Invention" is to educate readers on the history and uses of Silly Putty.

Author's purpose for "Making Rules for a Made-Up Game" is to entertain readers with a silly story about kids making up their own game.

Day 4 (page 171)
Answers should include details about something students created by accident, what it was used for, and how it was made.

Day 5 (page 172)
Games and instruction sheets will vary.

Unit 10

Week 1

Day 1 (page 173)
1. B 3. D
2. B 4. A

Day 2 (page 174)
1. B 3. C
2. B 4. D

Day 3 (page 175)
1. A 2. B
3. Pluto is similar because it also orbits the sun.
4. Orbit means to circle or revolve around something.

Day 4 (page 177)
1. A 3. D
2. D 4. B
5. Main idea: The International Space Station is like a city in space.
Details: Answers may include food, rest, or exercise in space.

Day 5 (page 178)
Answers will be yes or no, but must include reasons why students would or would not want to live on the space station.

Week 2

Day 1 (page 179)
1. B 3. A
2. C 4. C

Day 2 (page 180)
1. C 3. B
2. B 4. A

Day 3 (page 181)
1. B 2. C
3. They moved around by pretending they were swimming.
4. Answers should include how students would feel if they were Silas or Mariana.

Day 4 (page 183)
1. A 3. C
2. B 4. B
5. Beginning: They swam to the moon and climbed into a giant crater.
Middle: They went to Saturn and grabbed onto the rings and spun around.
End: They zoomed down, out of space, and back to the swings.

Answer Key *(cont.)*

Day 5 (page 184)

Answers should include what students would explore with Silas and Mariana, what adventures they would have, and a corresponding picture.

Week 3

Day 1 (page 186)

1. B
3. A
2. C
4. D

5. Answers should include if students think space is mysterious and reasons why or why not.

Day 2 (page 187)

Text	Space Words
Inside the Space Station	space, astronauts, Earth, space station
Exploring Space	moon, crater, weightless, Saturn
Space: A Haiku	space, sky, moon, stars, planets

Day 3 (page 188)

Setting drawing for "Inside the Space Station" should include the astronauts sleeping and/or exercising.

Setting drawing for "Exploring Space" should include the two kids coming back down toward Earth and back to the swings.

Day 4 (page 189)

Answers should include what they found interesting about space, any surprises, and another topic they would like to learn about in the future.

Day 5 (page 190)

Poems must follow the Haiku format of 5-7-5 syllables and include a corresponding picture.

Unit 11

Week 1

Day 1 (page 191)

1. B
3. C
2. C
4. B

Day 2 (page 192)

1. B
3. C
2. B
4. B

Day 3 (page 193)

1. C
2. C

3. Prepare yourself for the natural disasters that are most common in your area.

4. Possible answer: It is better to prepare and be ready than not to prepare and regret it.

Day 4 (page 195)

1. C
3. C
2. D
4. B

5. Graphic organizers should include 4 details about natural disasters, which will vary.

Day 5 (page 196)

Answers should include what information students found most interesting and what else they would like to learn.

Week 2

Day 1 (page 197)

1. B
3. A
2. D
4. B

Day 2 (page 198)

1. C
3. C
2. B
4. B

Day 3 (page 199)

1. D
2. C

3. The queen sent the worker ants to check on the colony.

4. Possible answers: try again, rebuild, find somewhere dry to start over

Day 4 (page 201)

1. C
3. C
2. B
4. B

5. Possible answers:

Queen	Ants
a good leader, prideful, wise	brave, tired, loyal
Both	
hard working, determined, helpful	

Day 5 (page 202)

Answers should include details about times students had to redo something and a comparison to the ants' experiences.

Week 3

Day 1 (page 204)

1. C
3. D
2. B
4. C

5. Possible answers: beanies, mittens, earmuffs, leg warmers, sweats, sweatshirts, etc.

Day 2 (page 205)

Example

Text	Words with a Prefix or Suffix
Rebuilding Together	reported, destroyed, worker, ruined, nonsense, rebuild, waited, expected, surprised, worked
Donation Station	coming, prepared

Answer Key *(cont.)*

Day 3 (page 206)

Possible answers for the Venn diagram:

Natural Disasters—nonfiction

Both—damage from natural disasters

Rebuilding Together—fictional characters, building ant colonies

Day 4 (page 207)

The central theme is about being prepared, not giving up, and working together to achieve a goal. Answers should include specific examples.

Day 5 (page 208)

Posters should include ways students can help their local communities.

Unit 12

Week 1

Day 1 (page 209)
1. C   3. A
2. D   4. A

Day 2 (page 210)
1. B   3. A
2. C   4. D

Day 3 (page 211)
1. B   2. A
3. The civil rights movement started because of Rosa Parks.
4. Answers might include feeling proud, scared, nervous, and/or brave.

Day 4 (page 213)
1. C   3. B
2. D   4. B
5. Answers should be in the chronological order of the text.

Day 5 (page 214)

Answers should be in friendly letter format and may include respect, forgiveness, acceptance, loyalty.

Week 2

Day 1 (page 215)
1. B   3. B
2. C   4. D

Day 2 (page 216)
1. A   3. C
2. B   4. A

Day 3 (page 217)
1. B   2. A
3. Lisa was worried a friend might laugh at her.
4. Answers should include what students would do if they were in Lisa's situation.

Day 4 (page 219)
1. B   3. A
2. C   4. B
5. Beginning: Lisa's teacher said she had a surprise and told Lisa to go outside.
Middle: Jackie Robinson helped Lisa work on her baseball skills.
End: Lisa woke up from her dream and made a commitment to never give up.

Day 5 (page 220)

Answers should describe a time when students didn't give up and compare it to Lisa's experience.

Week 3

Day 1 (page 222)
1. B   3. C
2. B   4. D
5. Noisemakers are not allowed because they would distract the ballplayers.

Day 2 (page 223)

Text	Baseball Words
An Inspirational Man	baseball, player, sports, athlete, strong, fast
A Magical Moment	game, catching, throwing, hitting, player, teams, professional
Ballpark Rules	ballbark, food, drinks, park

Day 3 (page 224)
1. Author's purpose for writing "An Inspirational Man" is to educate readers about Jackie Robinson and teach them to never give up.
2. Author's purpose for writing "A Magical Moment" is to entertain readers and teach a central message to never give up.

Day 4 (page 225)

Answers should include details about people students would like to meet and a corresponding picture.

Day 5 (page 226)

Students should write a list of rules for a place of their choosing.

Digital Resources

Accessing the Digital Resources

The digital resources can be downloaded by following these steps:

1. Go to **www.tcmpub.com/digital**

2. Use the 13-digit ISBN number to redeem the digital resources.

3. Respond to the question using the book.

4. Follow the prompts on the Content Cloud website to sign in or create a new account.

5. The content redeemed will appear on your My Content screen. Click on the product to look through the digital resources. All file resources are available for download. Select files can be previewed, opened, and shared.

For questions and assistance with your ISBN redemption, please contact Shell Education.

email: customerservice@tcmpub.com

phone: 800-858-7339

Contents of the Digital Resources

- Standards Correlations
- Writing Rubric
- Fluency Rubric
- Class and Individual Analysis Sheets